The Story of VICTOR VALLEY

Technology is wonderful but not quite perfect — the following pages are to correct imperfections in your book. We apologize for any inconvenience.

Heritage Media Corp.

EDWARD LEO LYMAN

Reginald Frost, British son-in-law of Brown-Verde Ranch owner, accompanied by cowhands Blue Thorpe and Ray Myers, working cattle at the ranch in 1916
Mohahve Historical Society

(Right and below)
Calf roper in Victorville Independence Day rodeo in 1920
Photo by Charles Mitchell
Mojave River Valley Museum

and hogs on the premises. While the Sterlings and Frosts operated the ranch, a considerable number of visitors, primarily from Redlands, made overnight and extended visits to the beautiful spot, clearly a forerunner to guest ranch endeavors of the future.

Throughout the 1900s, Victor Valley cattlemen continued to cooperate with each other and those in neighboring areas in annual roundup rodeos. Those in the late spring of 1911 was no exception. Cowhands from the Verde, along with other ranchers such as the Robinsons from Oro Grande, joined the roundup in the Lancaster area. An estimated 2,500 cattle were handled in the process, including far more calves than in the preceding year. Almost a month later, after similar operations in the Barstow vicinity, the so-called "rhodea" reached Oro Grande. The cowhands were particularly appreciative of the dinner, featuring fried chicken and ice cream, offered by the Bennette family, always genial hosts in that neighborhood. By late June, what observers considered the largest roundup in the history of the Mojave rangelands was about to conclude. There were substantial livestock increases despite the fact that open grazing lands were limited as more homestead lands were taken up.

As the cowboys were still gathered after their arduous roundup season, local organizers decided to stage a real rodeo as part of the Fourth of July celebration. Bronc riding had been a feature of the previous Victorville Independence Day celebrations, but the event in 1911 was probably the largest spectator-oriented rodeo staged in the region up to that time. The cowboys and onlookers arrived at the Brown-Verde Ranch early in the day. Horse racing was an inevitable event, as it would be for years thereafter in the area. But the special features of the day were what would become traditional rodeo contests, including bronc riding, steer riding and calf roping. After the cowboy contests were finished, the crowd, including many from Oro Grande and Hesperia, enjoyed ice cream and cake. Later that evening a dance was held at the Victorville Hall.

M. Penn Phillips, Hesperia developer, and his friend, former boxing champion Jack Dempsey, in 1954
Hesperia: A Pictorial History

Phillips, with an illustrious group of financial associates, purchased the largest private land parcel to change hands in Southern California in 35 years. This secured 20,000 acres from the Appleton Land, Water and Power Company and the associated Lacey estate, reportedly for $1.25 million. Planners expected the development process to cost an additional $7 million to properly prepare the 36-square-mile tract. Seasoned promoters expected a seven-year process to bring the project to full fruition using promotional ads aimed primarily at Los Angeles-area radio and television users, along with celebrity-presence attention similar to what Apple Valley had profited from. Longtime Phillips friend, former boxing champion Jack Dempsey, was particularly visible. Predictably, a new elementary school was soon needed and built.

Unfortunately, the aggressive sales tactics of some sales people led to complaints to the Public Utilities Commission and the California Bureau of Real Estate. The charges to the former, dealing with reportedly inadequate water service, were no longer Phillips' responsibility and would have to be resolved through a long struggle to gain public control of what had always been a private water company. Phillips and several of his sales staff were accused of pointing to commercial possibilities of certain lots despite zoning prohibitions. The company head argued he did not know of such practices if they occurred. But he was temporarily barred from selling real estate as were most of the others accused. Two were eventually banned from such sales for life. Phillips successfully withdrew from financial involvement with Hesperia at that point, but the stigma has, to some extent, remained connected to his name.

Community center at Lime Street Park, Hesperia, built by volunteer labor in the mid-1950s
Hesperia: A Pictorial History

San Bernardino County
Fair 1993 "pig races"
"Shades of Victor Valley," Victorville Branch, San Bernardino County Library, Ida Jean Green Collection

increasing in price from $17,000 at the end of the 1970s to as high as $140,000 just 10 years later. The number of vacant lots continues to diminish as residence construction has persisted through good and poor economic times. Permanent residents far outnumber weekend visitors and there is an ever increasing proportion of younger families locating there. Silver Lakes, near Helendale, draws on a similar format and appeal. The old Jess Ranch, converted from turkey production to its origins as a guest ranch, features a retirement community with age restrictions still rare in the high desert, though common in many other communities.

The last decade of the century started badly so far as maintaining previous prosperity and expansion was concerned. The value of buildings erected in 1990 dropped some 40 percent from the level of the previous year. And by 1994 the number of single-family homes constructed was less than one-third of that in 1989. To a small extent some residential building activity shifted to Adelanto, whose population jumped from 8,250 in 1990 to 12,050 in 1993. There had been but 14 homes built there in 1989, but this increased to 121 in 1990, 487 in 1991 and 966 in 1992. Adelanto civic leaders were more aggressive than other communities in attracting new businesses to their developing industrial park. This was impressive in comparison with their neighbors, particularly Hesperia, which was losing such firms at the same time. Unfortunately, at that point George Air Force Base closure became a reality for the high desert region. There is no way to discount the negative impact of the loss of 7,000 area jobs related to disbanding the facility that had done so much to stimulate recent growth in the valley.

As Victor Valley's phenomenal expansion got under way, a few farsighted leaders considered the possibilities of a unified city with one municipal government and school district. As an unmentioned precedent, the Riverside County towns of Edgemont, Sunnymead and Moreno were just then successfully consolidating into the booming municipality of Moreno Valley. There were numerous practical obstacles to such a move, some voiced in 1974 by longtime Victorville city councilman and mayor Terry Caldwell, amidst reports of the Local Agency Formation Commission hearing considerations of Victorville's water district annexing Hesperia into its service area. As some

Author's note in explanation of railroad photos.

As usual in publishing a book, amidst demanding deadlines, mistakes were made in The Story of Victor Valley. The copy and artistic editors got carried away copying images from the published works of the legendary Hesperia railroad historian, Chard Walker. He had graciously offered permission to copy the ones the author chose to use, but others were essentially added in end pages which were less authorized. They were also less than fair in not leaving the credits to Walker's books in the photo captions, along with the actual photographers.

The two books from which most railroad photos came are as follow:
Walker, Chard L. Railroading through Cajon Pass. Prototype Modeler, Inc.: Danvers, Me., 1978. (A. P. A.) below.
and
----. Chard Walker's Cajon: Rail Passage to the Pacific. Trans-Anglo Books: Glendale, California, 1985. (R. P. P.) below.

Endpapers: Photo by Alan Miller Aug. 7, 1985 in Cajon Canyon just above Sullivan's Curve. RPP

P. 3 Phot date was Oct. 8, 1950. Location between west Victorville and Thorn. RPP

P. Stan Kistler's photo was taken Feb 21, 1977 in Upper Mojave Narrows. RPP

P. 33 Lower photo was not a nineteenth century one by railroad builder, Fred Perris, as Steel Photo Service claimed, but one taken in 1948 by Lewis Harris.

P. 54 Lower photo was not taken at the original cement plant dedication as some assumed, but was a reenactment (fan excursion) taken Jan. 29, 1950.

Incidently, some of the flower filler pages were the art editor's choice, against the author's will. And scanning photos occasionally has horse races and other such things going in the wrong direction.

Leo Lyman

SF
5394
S F

First Edition

ISBN: 1-886483-47-7
Library of Congress Card Catalog Number: 00-103660
Author: Edward Leo Lyman
Publisher: C.E. Parks
Editor-in-Chief: Lori M. Parks
VP/National Sales Manager: Ray Spagnuolo
VP/Corporate Development: Bart Barica
CFO: Randall Peterson
Production Manager: Deborah Sherwood
Managing Editor: Betsy Baxter Blondin
Art Director: Gina Mancini
Senior Designer: Susie Passons
Production Staff: Jeff Caton, Brad Hartman, Dave Hermstead, Jay Kennedy, John Leyva, Marianne Mackie,
Bob Minton, Gavin Rattmann, Charlie Silvia
Project Editor: Elizabeth Lex
Coordinating Editors: Renee Kim, Betsy Lelja, Sara Rufner, Mary Ann Stabile, Adriane Wessels, John Woodward
Profile Writers: Elizabeth Cox, Gina Roquet
Human Resources Manager: Ellen Ruby
Administration: Juan Diaz, Debbie Hunter, Azalea Maes, Majka Penner, Scott Reid, Patrick Rucker, Cory Sottek

Published by

HERITAGE Media Corp.

Heritage Media Corp.
6354 Corte del Abeto, Suite B
Carlsbad, California 92009
www.heritagemedia.com

Printed by Heritage Media Corp. in the United States of America
Published in cooperation with the Mohahve Historical Society

Mohahve Historical Society

"Victor Valley, encompassing Adelanto, Apple Valley, Hesperia and Victorville, has a rich and colorful history."

Photo by Frank Peterson, Alan Miller Collection

Table of Contents

Preface

For someone who appreciates detail, relationships and explanations of historical causation as much as I do, few tasks are more difficult than drafting a brief sketch history of Victor Valley. Yet I understand brevity is of the essence in this book. It is not a completely balanced summary, since more pages were devoted to earlier and less-known periods, with later events somewhat slighted in comparison. Particular attention has been focused on the efforts to develop the water resources of the Mojave River and why they have never really worked, a mystery to most area residents.

For those who desire a more in-depth study of the history of Victor Valley, I am completing a lengthy manuscript on the same subject which will be published within the next two years, likely to treat all subjects mentioned herein with more than adequate detail. There will also be extensive footnote citations and source material references used in both the pictorial and detailed histories. These include numerous columns published in Los Angeles, San Bernardino and Victorville newspapers over the past 150 years. A preliminary draft of this manuscript, *History of Victor Valley,* is available for examination at Victor Valley College Library.

The most concerted earlier efforts to gather and publicize the history of the Victor Valley were by charter members of the Mohahve Historical Society founded in 1963. The early society members did an invaluable service by interviewing the pioneer generation in the high desert and gathering some of their photographs before they were all gone. Much of this work was published in five volumes of *Mohahve,* an excellent anthology of local history. Other society members have carried on the history promotion mission since that time, including semi-sponsorship of the present publication. Also a high percentage of the photo images reproduced herein, including those from the rare promotional booklets, *The Kingdom of the Sun,* come from the Mohahve collections. These materials are presently housed at Victor Valley College Library. I was not particularly active in the organization when this book project commenced and the society agreed to back the effort, but I am proud to now be serving as president of the Mohahve (Victor Valley) Historical Society which receives considerable proceeds from the sale of this work. Mohahve Historical Society members Richard Thompson and Larry Reese read this manuscript and markedly improved it. Fran Elgin, Mohahve Historical Society vice president, not only helped proofread, but as Victor Valley College librarian, assisted me with her usual efficiency in selecting many of the photographs used herein. Suzzana Oliver, head librarian of Victorville Branch Library, San Bernardino County, and Clifford Walker, founder of Mohave River Valley Museum, Barstow, also went far beyond the call of duty assisting with photos for this book. I, of course, remain responsible for any errors of commission and omission.

Victor Valley College Library Local History Collection

"Far more significant to California than the fur trappers was the use of the Old Spanish Trail as a trade route between Southern California and New Mexico..."

Photo by Stan Kistler

CHAPTER ONE 1770-1858

Native Americans, Hispanic Contact and the Major American Travel-Trade Route

(Opening photo)
This sketch of a channel-less swampy section above the Upper Mojave Narrows was drawn by surveyor Frank Lecouvreur and published in his native Germany in the 1850s. There was apparently no regular river channel through the present Spring Valley Lake-Mojave Narrows Regional Park area until the great flood of 1862.
From East Prussia to the Golden Gate
by Frank Lecouvreur

Anthropologists believe that for at least 10,000 years American Indians have inhabited the Mojave Desert. Little remains of the so-called Indians who immediately preceded European settlement of Victor Valley, the people known as desert Serrano, sometimes called Vanyume. This is primarily because those people virtually ceased to exist in the area even before the first white settlers arrived. While Serranos recognized common cultural characteristics among their group, they apparently never united in any political sense in which the concept of tribe is usually considered. Organized through clan membership, each included several villages, or rancherias, and the lands surrounding them, including locales to which they made trips as the various native foods became ready for gathering. A chief, called a kika, whose functions included determining the proper time and place for such activities, led these expeditions. He also performed other duties, including setting the time of various ceremonial observances and festivals. Each kika had a large ceremonial house, wood-framed and covered with tule or brush mats and sometimes mud. He also served as custodian of the sacred bundle of great ceremonial importance among the Serrano and neighboring peoples. Another important office, the paha, also participated in ceremonial observances and notified the people of when these would occur. Similarly, the tcaka or singer, knew the myths of creation and the clan songs. In many clan groups a healing shaman, whose power supposedly sprang from dreams and visions, cured by administering herbs, sucking and psychic means.

Serrano ceremonial house and residence of the kika-chief, larger than most regular dwellings but otherwise of similar construction
The Serrano Indians of Southern California
by Frank Johnston

Similar to most Southern California American Indian groups, the Serrano divided into two basic social units or moieties, the Tukum, or Wildcat, and the Wahilyam, or Coyote. A major function of this division was in marriage, with a wildcat able to marry a coyote, but not another wildcat. With so many people thus having cousins among the neighboring villages, much less likelihood existed for hostile conflict than was often the case elsewhere. The four clan divisions of the western Mojave Desert region also included the Kaiujam, which generally occupied the Victor Valley. This clan included the rancherias of Guapiabit in south Hesperia and

Atongaibit in Summit Valley, along with the lesser-known Nakaviat near the upper Mojave Narrows. The populations of these villages never exceeded more than a few hundred each.

As with most American Indians, private ownership of tools, weapons and food preparation materials existed, but the food gathering and hunting areas remained communally owned. However, practices persisted through which clans enjoying an abundance of certain resources shared them with friendly neighboring clans. Perhaps a part of the periodic fiesta activity among the Serrano are the several occasions recorded by observers when entire villages were almost vacant while the usual inhabitants visited neighboring food-gathering areas as guests in the quest for juniper berries, acorns and other foods. This clan-cooperative tradition may be one of the most impressive aspects of the lives of these American Indians. It certainly prevented the conflicts often leading to tribal wars among many other peoples, particularly during times of food scarcity.

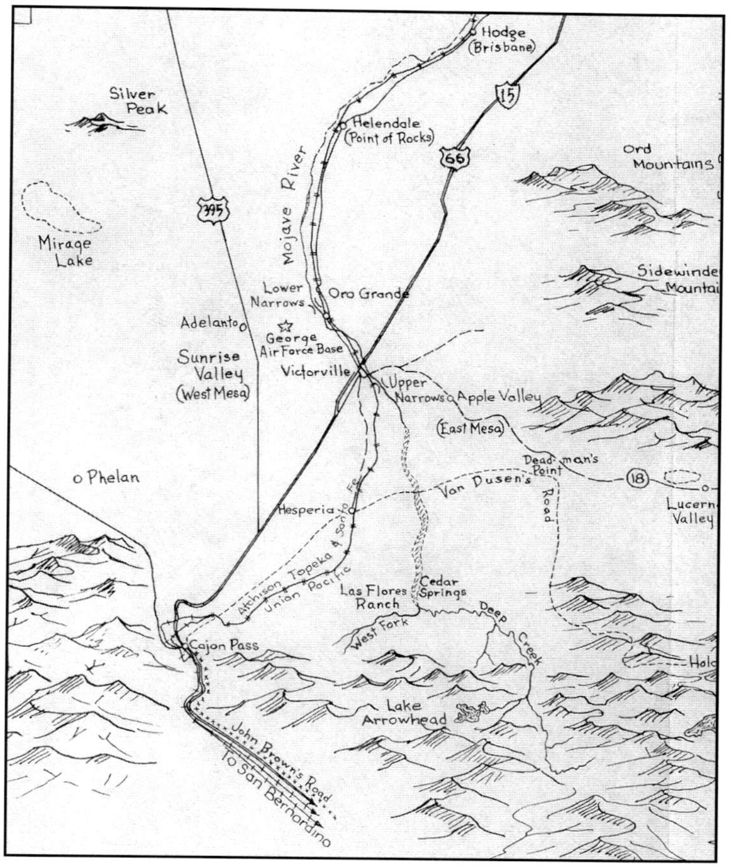

Map of Victor Valley created for Erma Peirson
The Mojave River and its Valley

Some observers have assumed the Mojave River Indians to be poor, but actually they had essentially solved the challenges of having sufficient food for comfortable living. In fact they appear to have enjoyed a greater variety than usual of staple foods. The good acorn-gathering areas along the northern slopes of the San Bernardino and San Gabriel mountains clearly did not belong just to those residing in closest proximity who enjoyed the bounty of the oak-abundant canyons. Both Father Francisco Garces and Jedediah S. Smith noted that those at least as far away as Barstow possessed supplies of the easily stored acorns. Pine nuts might have been a less consistent crop but still were often readily available in stands of pinion pine abundant in the area. Besides being a tasty and nourishing food roasted and taken right from the shell, Jed Smith described a mush served him and his men consisting of both acorns and pine nuts. He also mentioned a bread made from a small unidentified berry, which had the appearance of corn bread but tasted sweeter. What little evidence there is indicates this may have been made from berries of the juniper tree. Juniper trees were particularly abundant in the Mojave River area, and the berries, called wa'at among the American Indians, apparently remained an important, though presently little-known food. Early accounts of food gathering include large groups seeking supplies of this in the Hesperia area. Desert Indians also used mesquite beans and pods gathered in the deserts farther east and north of Victor Valley.

Another of the favorite foods consisted of the root and stock of the mescal, agave or yucca roasted in pits. Local American Indians also burned weeds and brush from areas to encourage a greater growth of chia grass, the seeds of which remained widely utilized as food. A rather unique food prized by the local American Indian residents was the sugar derived from the carrizo grass or cane apparently growing in abundance along the river bottoms near the upper and lower Mojave Narrows. Harvesting and processing methods are not clear, but early observers noted considerable use of the unique food. When Jedediah Smith visited the area, his local guides procured from a provision cache "something that resembled in appearance loaves of bread weighing 8 or 10 pounds. This proved so hard it required an ax to break it." Smith recorded "in taste it resembled sugar candy."

Early accounts also indicate that the forage along the Mojave River sustained an abundance of wild game. The American Indian name for the hills north of present Victorville on the east side of the Mojave River was Pat Kartz, which meant "mountain sheep mountain." American Indians hunted these animals, as did early white ranchers who eliminated them from the area. Jed Smith and his associates killed several antelope as they traveled through the valley in 1827. One group of Mormon gold seekers and missionaries hunting along the Mojave in 1849 killed at least four deer in but a few days. Water fowl, too, were abundant much of the year and certainly added to the impressive variety of the native diet.

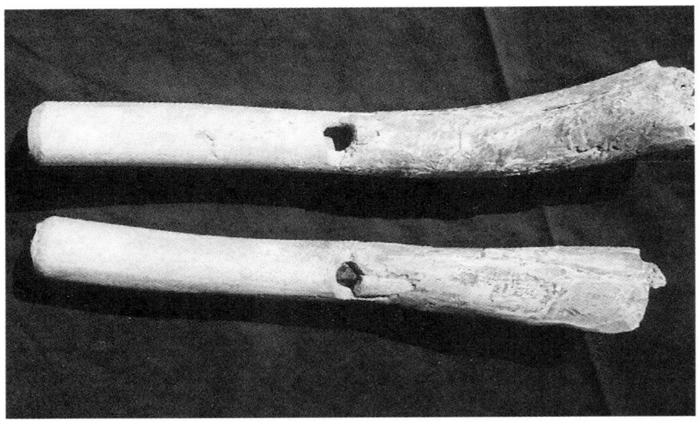
Bone flute-whistles found in Victor Valley area
Cambridge Museum

Rabbits undoubtedly loomed as the most important local game animal, both jack and cottontails, which the American Indians devised effective means of "harvesting." Jed Smith described his hosts preparing a rabbit feast. Extending a net 80 to 100 yards long in a place known to be thickly populated with the animals, they drove through the brush forcing the frightened game to run into the net. Then killing the two to three dozen rabbits soon entangled in the mesh, they cooked and offered them to the visiting mountain men. The Serranos also utilized snares, deadfall pits, throwing and digging sticks to obtain this usually abundant supply of food.

Rabbit skins were the main material for robes and blankets used during colder weather by American Indians living in the west Mojave area, although the skins of other small animals and deer were more widely used among the mountain Serranos. In warmer weather men wore breechclouts and women two-piece skirts, sometimes also fashioned from tree bark. They did considerable beadwork using shells, stones, bones and seeds and applied abundant tattooing to the upper bodies, as did the neighboring Mojave Indians. They fashioned sandals from plant fibers from which they also made the rabbit-catching nets and snares.

The Serranos manufactured considerable terra cotta pottery, covering many of their jars or ollas with freehand painted designs of dots, lines, triangles and concentric circles. They also fashioned baskets, bags, mats and other similar articles from a variety of reeds, weeds and grasses. These, too, included some geometric and band designs.

Most of the dwellings and other structures were made of brush and tule mats shaped like an inverted cup on a willow frame built over a round excavation about two feet deep and 10 feet across. The ceremonial houses were larger but constructed similarly. Their round storage containers were made of willow or tule and upraised on four legs.

Serrano entertainment included storytelling, singing, games and combinations thereof such as singing accompanied by the peon gambling game, in which two teams of four people tried to outguess each other as to which held the object in his closed fist. Music was made with whistles of bone and from wooden flutes, along with rattles created by attaching two turtle shells with pebbles inside. Rituals, including burials to the neck in a heated pit, were performed on the mother and baby at childbirth and the time of a girl's coming of age. The boy's initiation included visions and dreams induced by a drink made from jimson weed, followed by dancing around a fire in the ceremonial house until overcome by the effects of the drug. The visions and interpretations by the paha and shamans supposedly guided the young men in their future life. During this period the older men, shamans and tcaka taught the boys various songs.

The Mojave River had long functioned as part of a major trade route between the Pacific Coast and the Pueblo Indian villages of Arizona and New Mexico. The Mojave Indians residing along the Colorado River served as the primary carriers of this trade. There were occasional conflicts between the desert Serranos and the Mojaves, but it is also clear that they carried on extensive trade with each other. The Serrano chief first encountered by Father Garces possessed impressive wealth in beads undoubtedly brought from the seacoast by the Mojaves. Later, the Serranos apparently enlisted their neighbors in their contemplated conflict with Hispanic soldiers near the San Gabriel Mission through payment in shell beads.

Mohave Indian runners, Panambona and Mitiwara, photographed during Lt. George Wheeler's expedition to the Colorado River, 1871
Victor Valley College Library Local History Collection, donated by Jean Goldbrandsen

The coming of the first Europeans into Serrano territory brought far greater impact than any other factor on the lives of the native desert inhabitants. Father Junipero Serra established the first mission in Upper California at San Diego in 1769. His corps of dedicated Franciscan missionaries aiming to Christianize the California Indians soon established a chain of missions. A supply route to these by land soon proved essential. The viceroy of New Spain assigned Sonora frontiersman, Juan Bautista de Anza, to locate a road from Mexico to California. After ultimate success, the same leader received assignment to lead a colonization company over the route.

One of the missionaries on these trips, Father Francisco Garces, had already devoted much time and energy to exploring in present Arizona. Seldom in the annals of heroic Hispanic exploration was there a figure to equal Garces, totally dedicated to his lifework of preaching his version of Christianity to American Indians. One associate missionary, Pedro Font, described Garces as well suited for his lifework asserting his disposition to be like an American Indian himself, "phlegmatic in everything." Font said the Father sat with the American Indians around the fire with his legs crossed, musing two or three hours or more, "oblivious to everything else, talking with them with much serenity and deliberation." The describing diarist also mentioned "although the foods of the Indians are as nasty and dirty as those outlandish people themselves, the Father eats them with great gusto and says that they are good for the stomach and very fine." Father Font concluded that God had created Garces "solely for the purpose of seeking out these unhappy, ignorant, and rustic people."

In late 1775 Garces left the deAnza expedition and headed north to visit among the Mojave Indians near present Needles. Thereafter, with Mojave guides the Franciscan explorer traversed the east Mojave Desert following the well-traveled trail entering Serrano territory east of the Mojave River sink. After traveling up the Mojave past several small rancherias and abandoned village sites, Garces encountered large numbers of Mojave River Indians near present Barstow. The Father received

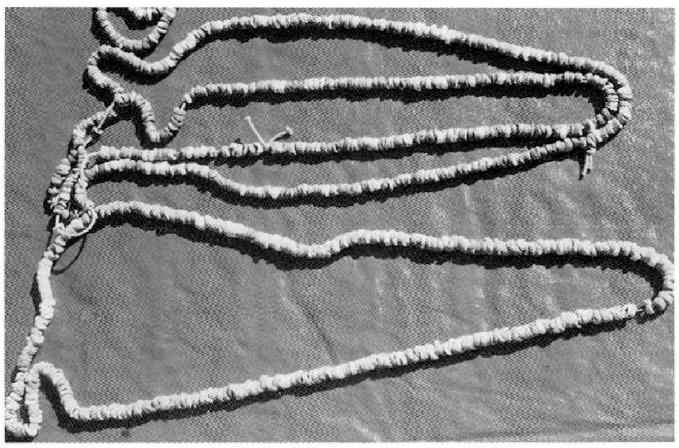

Shell beads, probably from the Santa Barbara channel region, traded to Mojave River Indians and later found in that vicinity
Cambridge Museum

Franciscan missionaries and associates exploring what became the Old Spanish Trail
Rendered by Paul Salisbury in ***Utah: The Right Place*** *by Thomas G. Alexander*

greetings from the chief of several rancherias he had passed while at a village near present Helendale. The chief presented Garces with a string of seashell beads some two yards long, and one of the chief's wives poured acorns over Garces' head then threw away the basket. The conspicuous display of expendable wealth duly convinced the missionary that these American Indians did not suffer from the poverty he had expected of them. Although the Garces visit to the Victor Valley did not lead to the establishment of a mission, his efforts as the first European explorer of the area looms as sufficiently significant that his memory should be permanently preserved, although the movement to erect that memorial has not yet materialized.

The missionaries regarded the continued presence farther inland from the California missions of a large body of American Indians not yet brought under the discipline of the mission system as a major negative influence. Partly for this reason, the Franciscans projected a second chain of interior missions to be planted after getting the coastal missions fully established. In the process of investigating for suitable sites, an expedition including Father Jose Maria Zalvidea entered the western Mojave Desert region in 1806. The exploring missionaries traveled eastward along a well-established American Indian trail to the village of Atongai, in present east Hesperia. Here Zalvidea baptized five elderly Serranos, the first known Christian sacraments to be performed in future San Bernardino County. After baptizing two more at nearby Guapiabit, the missionaries departed toward the San Bernardino Valley.

Although there was no other known missionary penetration of the western Mojave region, records at the closest missions of San Gabriel and San Fernando indicate converts from the Mojave River villages. After the missions began to lose population to epidemics and individual abandonments, the padres clearly increased efforts to attract greater numbers of American Indians from the more distant areas. More than 20 from Atongai alone show in the records as coming to the San Fernando mission between 1809 and 1812. However, the Spanish military authorities who usually accompanied the missionaries never fully brought the region under their control. On the contrary, the area beyond the San Gabriel-San Bernardino mountains became a haven for escaped mission residents alienated from the rigid discipline and perhaps seemingly unfair treatment experienced there. Since practicing Roman Catholics believed that those abandoning religious commitments after baptism risked eternal damnation, they assumed the obligation to bring the lost souls back to the missions.

In 1808 a military party seeking escaped American Indians approached the Victor Valley from the east. When Commander Palomares encountered numerous Serranos congregated to gather acorns in the upper Cajon Pass, he sent an emissary to the chiefs explaining he had a list of escapees he wished to return to the mission. The chiefs rejected the request recalling that when they had previously accepted an offer to receive bolts of cloth in exchange for returned runaways from the San Gabriel mission, they had instead been seized and whipped daily for more than a week. Recognizing the futility of expecting cooperation, Palomares moved on through the Cajon Pass toward the San Gabriel area, where he had less trouble capturing escapees remaining closer to the missions.

After the Mexican Revolution began in September 1810, government support for the California military establishment almost disappeared. What few soldiers remained could hardly defend the missions and could not be expected to venture into the frontier sanctuaries of escaped American Indians. That same year saw an allied body of Serrano, Mojave and other American Indians attack the San Gabriel mission, with warriors approaching within a short distance of the objective before being thwarted. The crisis persisted throughout the year. Some former mission Amercian Indians abandoned San Gabriel and it is evident that even several years later numerous escaped American Indians remained absent, some having taken refuge in the Mojave Desert.

In 1819 Southern Californians were again seized by panic over possible war with the Mojave Indians and perhaps their allies after several traders of the Mojave tribe were killed by guards at Mission San Buenaventura. This time the California military took some initiative, marching down the upper Mojave River in November. Father Joaquin Nuez, chaplain and diarist of the expedition, noted that some local American Indians had obviously displeased the hostile Mojaves and had been killed. At least some of the half-dozen victims were neophytes in Christianity. Nuez and his associates gave the victims a proper burial near the Upper Narrows, erecting a large cross to mark the spot.

At the same time Garces blazed a new overland trail from the Colorado River into Southern California, counterpart Franciscan missionaries based in New Mexico were similarly engaged far to the north and east. Fathers Atanasio Domingues and Sylvestre de Escalante opened a route from Taos, New Mexico, into the middle of present-day Utah. Not until 50 years later, in 1826, did these two route segments of what became known as the Old Spanish Trail become effectively linked. This was attributed to the greatest of the Anglo-American explorers of the Far West, Jedediah Strong Smith. Engaged in the quest for beaver pelts, Smith, a fur company official, ventured into the uncharted region to the southwest of the usual Rocky Mountain trapping area. After leaving future Utah and crossing the corner of present Arizona, Smith's brigade passed Las Vegas in future Nevada, then traveled down the Colorado River to Needles, thereby joining the portions

American Indian dwellings situated adjacent to Mission San Gabriel Arcangel were used by Christians new to the faith, including a considerable number from Victor Valley Serrano rancherias.
California's Gabrielino Indians
by Bernice Eastman Johnston

Painting of Jed Smith and his men crossing the Mojave Desert in 1826 as depicted in this painting by Charles Russell now at the New York Public Library

Pack mule caravan similar to those traveling annually over the Old Spanish Trail from Los Angeles through Victor Valley to Santa Fe
Old Spanish Trail
by LeRoy R. Hafen

of the Old Spanish Trail. Although he also discovered other important trails of the West, his southwestern expedition, repeated the following year, stands among his most significant accomplishments. His diary accounts of travels up the Mojave River in 1826 and 1827 provide valuable information on the Serrano Indian inhabitants not otherwise available.

While Smith and his men trapped and explored, other equally venturesome Taos, New Mexico-based mountain men from several nations engaged similarly in future Arizona. In this process they antagonized more than a few of the local American Indians, which soon led to trouble for Smith and many others. Three years after the opening of the new overland trail, three rival groups of fur trappers traveled over it into Southern California. The first party, led by Ewing Young and including young Kit Carson, took the trail after trapping across Arizona. Thomas "Pegleg" Smith, with a separate brigade of Anglo-Americans, also passed over the trail about the same time. And the British fur trapper-explorer, Peter Skene Ogden, led an expedition of Hudson's Bay Company men through that area, perhaps sent to gain further information other than what Jed Smith had reported when recently in the Oregon center of Hudson's Bay operations. Company policy was to discourage others from penetrating Hudson's Bay domain. After Ogden's report the Hudson's bay Company probably assumed no threat from Southern California.

Far more significant to California than the fur trappers was the use of the Old Spanish Trail as a trade route between Southern California and New Mexico and to other regions in the United States. The first to use the general route for transporting trade goods, traveling southwest from Las Vegas instead of back to the Colorado River and Needles, was Antonio Armijo in 1829-30. His party brought woolen blankets and serapes from New Mexico to exchange for horses and mules in California that were driven back to the trader's home area at profits of up to 500 percent over the California cost. William Wolfskill and George C. Yount, naturalized Mexican citizens originally from the American South, led the first party to journey the entire length of what became the main trail in 1830-31. They, too, brought woolen goods from New Mexico, which also reaped satisfactory profits.

For the next 15 years frequent trading expeditions continued over the trail, with some evidence that they occurred annually. In April 1842 at least 4,450 head of legally acquired animals departed for New Mexico via the Cajon Pass. But it soon developed that it was more profitable to secure California livestock for their return trip by illegal means rather than through purchase or trade. The traffic in stolen livestock compelled Los Angeles officials to institute inspection measures for eastern-bound animals.

The legitimate and other livestock driving ventures invariably utilized the abundant natural pastures along the Mojave River, recouping animal strength for the arduous desert crossing.

By the 1840s, as the fur trade declined, several Anglo-American trappers also engaged in horse and mule stealing. Old Bill Williams, Pegleg Smith and Jim Beckwourth were all linked to successful ventures of this kind, the former in connection with Ute Chief Wakara and his braves, allegedly gathering some 3,000 head of animals for sale farther north and east. The latter marketed some of his stolen animals as far away as eastern Colorado. Wakara was perhaps the most successful horse thief in the history of the region. It is for him that Horsethief Canyon, a portion of present Summit Valley, was named.

Hispanic vaqueros herding horses — typical of the extensive activity along the Old Spanish Trail through Victor Valley by both legitimate traders and numerous horse thieves
The Cattle on a Thousand Hills
by Robert Glass Cleland
The Huntington Library, Art Collections, & Botanical Gardens

It was largely to protect Southern California livestock from such raids that the first settlement in the San Bernardino area, made up of former residents of New Mexico, was established. Led by Lorenzo Trujillo, these men soon figured in expeditions into the Victor Valley. Mexican governor of California, Pio Pico, assigned Benjamin "Benito" Wilson, veteran of the Old Spanish Trail, to lead a campaign against a band of renegade American Indians established on the Mojave River who were making periodic raids on livestock in the Southland. Arriving at the Mojave River, the commander, who was riding in advance of his main force, sighted four American Indians approaching who had not seen him. Intending to capture them in hopes of gaining information, he hid until they were close at hand. Coincidentally, one of the American Indians proved to be Joaquin, leader of the renegades the party sought. He had once served as a page at Mission San Gabriel Arcangel, but brutal treatment by the mayordomo of Rancho del Chino, then still in mission hands, had deeply embittered him toward the Spaniards. At first Joaquin assumed Wilson to be simply a traveler but soon recognized that the military campaign was after him and his men. He immediately snatched a poisoned arrow and prepared to shoot, which left Wilson no choice but to also shoot. Both discharged their weapons simultaneously, with Wilson hit in the shoulder and Joaquin in the breast. The wounded renegade leader lay cursing the Spaniards while his three companions fought to the death against Wilson's men, who arrived just in time to save him. Joaquin, too, was killed, after which Wilson rode to the river's edge where his faithful companion, Lorenzo Trujillo, sucked the poison from his wound and probably saved his life.

Early photograph of Paiute Indians camped along the Old Spanish Trail
Utah: The Right Place
by Thomas G. Alexander

Wilson dispatched most of his men against the other American Indians, whom they found barricaded on a rocky hillside. Fighting throughout the day, the Californians failed to take the position. Later Wilson again led his troops into the Mojave River country and this time they surrounded the American Indian stronghold. When those besieged refused to surrender, the fighting continued until all the American Indian men had been killed. The women and children were taken to the San Bernardino Valley, but eventually Governor Pico ordered them released on the grounds that they may not have abandoned the mission and neighboring ranches of their own free will.

Undoubtedly some former residents of the Mojave River region returned to their homelands

Accompanying artist Edward Kern's scene of preparation of Fremont party for a day's march — guide Kit Carson would shout "catch up" as a wake-up call and virtually leave stragglers not ready at the proper time.
Fremont: Explorer for a Restless Nation
by Ferol Egan

after the demise of the missions, but their history is essentially unrecorded. One major challenge was the large traffic of outside traders and travelers, many of whom regarded all American Indians as hostile enemies. Another problem for the longtime American Indian inhabitants was the apparent culmination of the long-developing process of Takic-speaking southern Paiute or Chemhuevi Indians, formerly residents of the relatively more harsh and food-scarce lands to the north, moving into the areas left at least partially vacant by the desert Serranos. Violent confrontations between the two groups remain unrecorded in the known sources. Then, too, there were the European-carried diseases to which local American Indians had no immunity. Records indicate that an influenza epidemic in 1832, along with three of smallpox in 1844, 1862-3, and the 1870s, took a horrible toll. According to Tomas, one of the surviving American Indians interviewed by ethnologist John P. Harrington in about 1900, "... the viruelas [smallpox] came 3 times and killed all the Serranos. The people tried to run away but died on the road and the coyote ate them — men, women, and children... Before these epidemics the Serranos were very numerous..."

Among other historically significant journeys over the Old Spanish Trail was a group of two dozen men, mostly Anglo-Americans led by William Workman and John Rowland. They came to California with the annual overland trade expedition of 1841, but with the avowed purpose of establishing permanent homes. With a similar group arriving over the Oregon-California Trail, this commenced an inflow of Anglo-American emigration which would soon become a considerable flood.

Another event symbolic of the impending transition of California from Mexican province to an important part of the United States was the journey of government explorer John Charles Fremont. He passed through the Mojave River Valley on the return portion of his second expedition into the Far West. Guided by Kit Carson, the party sought the Old Spanish Trail, which headed in precisely the direction Fremont intended to go to strike the Colorado Rockies at the point he wished. Fremont's party reached the Mojave River near present Oro Grande on April 20, 1844, and appreciated the roadway that made travel markedly easier for the horses. Fremont's description of the river and its lush growth of cottonwood trees is one of the best of the area just as it was about to become a part of the United States through the Treaty of Guadalupe-Hidalgo.

Excellent (after brush fire) view of the road excavated on the side of the ridge-ramp wagon road up and down the Cajon Pass "hogback" constructed by W. T. B. Sanford for freight and pioneer wagons in 1850 and used until 1855
Mohahve III

In 1848, the first year of United States possession of Southern California, Mormon soldiers who had assisted with garrison duty after the Mexican War brought the first wagon up the Cajon Pass and overland to Utah.

Thereafter several Mormon Battalion veterans like Jefferson Hunt led other American emigrants over that all-season route to the gold fields, making this southern route a heavily traveled road. While there were few fatalities on the desert route, Isaac Williams, a rancher in Chino, took impressive responsibility to send supplies and assist travelers who were out of food and exhausted at the end of the arduous journey. He or the men he sent usually met the struggling emigrants along the Mojave River, particularly in 1849 and 1850. In 1851 a company of 437 Mormons traveled over the route to establish a colony at San Bernardino. Traffic between there and Utah would remain heavy for the remainder of the decade. This included a large volume of freight, particularly in 1859, when at least 270 heavily loaded wagons passed down the Mojave en route to Salt Lake City in a three-month period. There was also a monthly mail service by horse and mule during most of the decade.

By that time there were also government surveyors on the desert seeking the best railroad routes as well as dividing the land into sections and townships for sale. Lt. Amiel W. Whipple commented on the valley of the Mojave in his 1856 report describing "much fertile land on the banks of this stream which sustains a vigorous growth of grass and willow." This account was the first good publicity on the area.

During the terrible drought in Southern California in 1856, some ranchers saved their livestock by driving their herds up the Cajon Pass to pasture along the Mojave River. In June the Los Angeles *Star* reported "large bands of cattle have been driven out on the Mohave, the grass being abundant." This was the first known Anglo-American utilization of Victor Valley rangelands other than by passing emigrants.

In 1855 George W. Bean, one of the Mormons who helped establish an Indian mission in Las Vegas, noted while on a trip to San Bernardino that there were prospectors seeking gold along the Mojave River. Although there is no evidence of success, church members did find gold in considerable quantities in the San Bernardino Mountains, particularly north of future Big Bear Lake at what would later be named Holcomb Valley. The main route utilized to reach these placer mines was by way of the Cajon Pass and then along the road later named after Jed Van Dusen through Victor Valley. One of the most persistent prospectors, Theodore Turley, located a mine of placer gold in "the canyon that goes to the Mojave," which would place it somewhere in or near Summit Valley, probably in the area still known as "Mormon Diggings." The most dedicated Mormons abandoned the area in 1857-58 before much mining success could be enjoyed.

During the winter of 1857-58, church leader Brigham Young made it known that he desired faithful Mormons to return to Utah to assist in the crisis of a United States Army invasion presumably to punish defiant church members. The abandonment of the San Bernardino community proved prompt and efficient. Many of those who left in haste concluded to remain along the Mojave while their livestock gained strength for the arduous desert crossing. One *Star* account mentioned a hundred wagon loads of emigrants waiting on the river for their time to cross the forbidding wasteland. The newspaper writer doubtless took considerable literary license in stating about 50 marriages had been performed within the camps and that some 25 babies had been born, although there were considerable numbers of both events. It is possible the name Mormon Crossing at later Sixth and D streets in Victorville stemmed partly from this extended camp at these best-river pasturelands.

Emigration to the Western Country, c. 1850
Utah: The Struggle for Statehood
by Ken Verdoia

2 CHAPTER TWO 1858-1880

Frontier Outpost to Mining and Milling Center

(Opening photo)
Original log structures built at Lane's Crossing in 1858-1859
Photo by d'Heureuse, 1863
The Bancroft Library
University of California, Berkeley

In 1858 Aaron G. Lane, a veteran of the Mexican War and California Gold Rush, established a ranch and way station on the west bank of the Mojave River at what was then called the last crossing. While there was a similar outpost called the Mormon Grocery operating farther downstream near Barstow as early as 1855, Lane's operation proved sufficiently durable to earn him designation as the first permanent settler in the area. Yet he did not have an auspicious start. In May 1859, Lane and his employees were "overpowered by Indians" reportedly "dispossessing the occupants of all their worldly goods." The Los Angeles *Star* took the occasion to argue that for far more military visibility was necessary in the desert region. Just prior to this time the U.S. Army had established Fort Mojave near Needles on the Colorado River, with much of its supply coming by freight wagons through Victor Valley.

Early the next year the *Star* reported that people, mainly from Texas and Utah, were settling along the Mojave. One of the settlers was young Silas Cox, who with three cowhand companions built "a little cabin out of small willow and cottonwood logs, and covered it principally of raw hides" at a riverbank location probably just south of present Jess Ranch. Members of the Bemis and Hancock families, formerly of Mormon San Bernardino, along with Aaron Lane, were also among those known to be pasturing cattle along the Mojave in 1860. Lane had a neighbor named Joseph Highmore establishing a land claim by that time. However, he most apparently left by year's end because of American Indian threats.

These difficulties commenced early in 1860 when Robert Wilburn, a foreman of a group of wranglers herding cattle for Los Angeles merchant Felix Bachman, was ambushed while searching for stolen stock. While it is impossible to establish who the perpetrators were, some concluded them to be Paiutes from Nevada or Utah. One such American Indian was later illegally executed for the crime in central Utah.

Camp Cady in 1863, built during the Carleton campaign against the Paiutes in 1860
Photo by d'Heureuse
The Bancroft Library
University of California, Berkeley

Later in the spring two Utah freighters, Thomas Williams and Parmeno "Jehu" Jackman were also killed by American Indians in the Bitter Springs area of what would later be called Fort Irwin Army Training Base.

These murders spurred further demands for military occupation of the Mojave region. Maj. James H. Carleton was promptly dispatched with troops to search the entire desert, ordered to "chastise" whatever American Indians were found. Five were killed during this campaign and a fort, Camp Cady, was established on the Mojave River just north of present Newberry Springs. The fort was soon abandoned until after the Civil War and when reoccupied, this outpost would have to be supplied by freight wagon traffic through the Cajon and Victor valleys.

By this time the original Serrano inhabitants of the Mojave River area had retreated to safer havens off the main roads or succumbed to European-carried diseases. They were gradually replaced by Paiute Indians, including Chemuhevis, from farther north. Capt. Winfield S. Hancock, later hero of the Battle of Gettysburg, perceptively recognized in 1860 that while the Paiutes had rarely been seen previously near the roadway along the Mojave River, they were by that point frequenting the area with far greater persistence. And while temporarily cowed by Carleton, when a promised military force did not return to the area the ensuing year, the American Indians there commenced demonstrating more defiance and hostility.

In 1861 a major gold rush commenced to Holcomb Valley, just north of present Big Bear Lake. It attracted a large influx of miners and freighters by the same route to the booming camps used by Mormon miners a few years previously. Blacksmith Jed Van Dusen was soon engaged to grade a better road from the northwestern corner of the mountain valley down the natural grade to later Victor Valley and across to the summit of Cajon Pass. There the road met another one being constructed by former mountain man John Brown and his partners, who had been authorized by the state legislature to establish a crucial toll road up the pass. When completed, these proved adequate when a heavy steam boiler and other equipment were successfully hauled over both roads for use in Holcomb Valley.

Near the end of the same year when the American Civil War erupted, Brown journeyed to Los Angeles where he secured a contract to provide U.S. Army troops stationed in the San Bernardino County area with beef and perhaps feed for their livestock. Providing these may have been the Brown family's initial motivation for utilizing the lush meadowlands above the Mojave Narrows, where his sons later established a permanent ranch in 1867, eventually called the Verde.

While the war yet raged, another drought in the California southland again forced ranchers, including William Wolfskill, to drive their cattle to the Mojave. One cowhand, J.E. Pleasants, later recalled helping herd 3,000 plus horses through the Cajon to a point on the river below Lane's Crossing. He noted that by then there was another way station operated by an easy-going Englishman, Nicholson, farther downstream. Because there were then so many freight wagon teams and drivers passing by, Pleasants asserted the wranglers were hardly lonely during the time they spent on the river. He also noted friendly relations with American Indians in the area.

Soon after the Civil War, passing emigrants brought four Paiute boys, sick or starving, to San Bernardino where they remained with foster families. Later, one of these was hunting rabbits with his adopted brothers when an argument ensued with boys from an aggressive Texan

Nicholson family's Point of Rocks home built in 1861
Photo by D'Heureuse
The Bancroft Library
University of California, Berkeley

Mule team and wagons used for hauling ore from desert mines of San Bernardino County
Photo by Seymour Alf
Mohave River Valley Museum, Barstow

family that recently arrived in the area. When a Texan youth pointed a gun at the American Indian, the latter instinctively aimed and fired his own weapon. An inquest concluded the incident to be a tragic accident. But a few months later, the community negligently allowed brothers and friends of the dead boy to take the American Indians back to their homes. While descending the north side of the San Bernardino Mountains, suspecting foul play, the boy who had killed the brother slipped away into the trees. Soon thereafter, he witnessed his fellow American Indians being murdered and beheaded by the other men.

Less than a month later, a cattle roundup was being conducted at what eventually became part of the Las Flores Ranch, in the same area as the killing of the three American Indian boys. During a windstorm, three of the cowhands, Nephi Bemis, Ed Parrish and Pratt Whitesides, were shot from ambush as they were seeking cattle in thickets near the Mojave River northeast of the ranchhouse. The bodies were retrieved and taken by fellow cowhands to San Bernardino for the largest funeral yet held there. While there was no known connection made between the two murderous incidents and no immediate retaliation against American Indians, it was later ascertained that Paiutes as far away as Utah knew of the killings and explained that the deaths of the cowboys were in retaliation for the death of the American Indian youths.

Early the following year, after an alleged American Indian looting of a mountain lumber camp, county citizens organized their own posse to pursue the supposed American Indian culprits. As the "army of the Mojave" searched for the camp of their presumed enemy, they discovered a fresh American Indian trail heading for Rabbit Springs on the edge of present Lucerne Valley. The self-appointed army moved closer, and on about February 18, staged a poorly coordinated attack from two directions that led to a fight lasting more than a full day. Four warriors were left dead on the battlefield and up to five women and children temporarily captured. Two of the so-called "rangers" were seriously wounded. Concern for them and the severe cold led to curtailing any further campaign at that time. Despite later boasting by many participants it is doubtful if the American Indians attacked were either the ones guilty of earlier raids or whether they understood the reason for being punished.

Two months later a group of miners from the temporarily flourishing Cushenbury City, about four miles southeast of the earlier battle site, killed all seven warriors caught sleeping. Among the trophies taken was a watch wheel implanted in the stock of a gun which was supposedly recognized to have belonged to one of the victims of the Las Flores killings, Ed Parrish. A similar claim had been made after the battle near Rabbit Springs, certainly intended to convey the impression, justified or not, that the American Indians deserved their fate.

Doubtful as it is that any of the American Indian victims were guilty of the crimes for which they were punished, it is absolutely certain that the other man meeting death in this chain of tragedy was entirely innocent. In March 1869 Franklin D. Woolley, a Utah merchant leading a wagon train loaded with goods through the Victor Valley, had several of his horses stray in the night. In search of them he went to Las Flores Ranch, where the animals had been pastured the previous season. Caught that night by rain, he awakened to find himself surrounded by Paiute warriors who killed him as he sought to escape. It was later established that this death resulted simply from the man being caught at a place some American Indians had decreed no European would occupy after the three American Indian boys had been killed there.

During the period of peak interest, as the first transcontinental railroad was being completed in 1868 and 1869, another such line was projected along the 35th parallel for entry into Southern California through Cajon Pass. Max Strobel, mayor of Anaheim, but also familiar with the Mojave River area, purchased almost 9,000 acres of land in what would later be Hesperia. He and fellow German emigrants could thereby control the railroad access to the California southland. At that time a San Bernardino correspondent to the Los Angeles *Star* reported "quite a rage for taking up government lands" during the first of several speculative boom periods in the high desert. But when the anticipated railroad construction became indefinitely delayed, the frenzy quickly faded.

Shown here are workmen handling silver bullion from a Mojave Desert region reduction mill. Bullion was hauled by freight wagons before the railroad. *Victor Valley College Library Local History Collection*

The renewed presence of military outposts in the desert assured major freight wagon traffic, soon dramatically enhanced by the demands of ever-expanding mining districts. An observer in early 1867 noted 43 outbound teams and wagons in one day between San Bernardino and Lane's Crossing. The expense of hauling virtually everything the men and animals ate or used remained massive. Barley that cost 2 cents a pound at the seaport of Wilmington cost 13 additional cents by the time it reached Camp Rock Springs, midway between Camp Cady and the Colorado River. This offered great opportunity to those in San Bernardino and soon, for

An ore processing plant was reassembled at several Mojave Desert locations and effective in reducing silver and related metals to more compact form for shipment to more sophisticated refineries beyond the region. *Victor Valley College Library Local History Collection*

settlers along the Mojave River to produce food, feed and other items and market them competitively without such high transportation costs.

Certainly the key to the freighting business flourishing through the Victor Valley and beyond was the development

Upper Toll Station in Cajon Pass built by John Brown and long operated by James Fears
Photo by d'Heureuse, 1863
The Bancroft Library
University of California, Berkeley

of at least a half-dozen desert mining areas not only in San Bernardino County but also in adjacent Inyo County and in Arizona. The first was the Clark Mountain District on the California-Nevada boundary. Up to 300 miners clustered around the principal town of Ivanpah. Some ore was reduced locally by primitive arrastra milling methods. Eventually a modern mill was installed, after which the main return cargo, hauled mostly by freighter and Victor Valley ranch owner Horace Clark, was silver bullion. One newspaper report in 1873 mentioned 12,000 pounds of high-grade ore shipped out in one freighting trip.

The New York Mountains Mining District, active briefly prior to the Civil War, reopened and boomed just south and east of Clark. Similar camps were established much farther south and west in the Ord Mountains and future Twenty-nine Palms areas, also at least partially supplied through Cajon Pass. And the first major mining district of the region, Holcomb Valley, enjoyed a revival of activity in the 1870s, with promising gold-bearing deposits on the extreme eastern edge, some purchased by famous mining and land speculator E.J. "Lucky" Baldwin.

The pioneer way station proprietor, Aaron Lane, had persistently resumed and expanded his operations despite difficulties with American Indians and a dispute with neighbors over property boundaries and titles. At the time that a fire destroyed his second station in late 1867, his yards were reportedly "crammed" with "immense" crops of hay, barley and corn he had produced there. After rebuilding the following season, Lane boasted to a San Bernardino newspaper that the soil at his establishment was "exceedingly fertile" and usually sufficiently moist to produce crops without irrigation. He often sent vegetables from his garden to the city to demonstrate the productivity of his domain.

Soon after the upper John Brown toll station was established near the top of the east Cajon Pass in Crowder Canyon, it was deemed necessary to construct another toll station to more effectively collect fees from travelers in the unavoidable narrow confines of Blue Cut below where the western routes down the pass converged. Son-in-law Sidney Waite and his bride, Matilda, operated the upper station. They soon added a "bar room," from which a large volume of Barton vineyards wine was dispensed. After several years, including serious incidents with American Indians, new proprietor Jim Fears and his wife took control and made the station equally popular because of the meals served, featuring locally procured venison steaks. An added incentive for patrons to avail themselves of the snug sleeping accommodations and tight corals for the draft animals was protection from the continued presence of numerous California grizzly bears in the vicinity. The river route always had several other way stations beyond Lane's including the Cottonwoods near future Hodge, probably the most popular on the river.

The first known operators of the several way stations at Mormon-Huntington Crossing, near present Sixth and D streets in Victorville, were members of the Burton family, relatives of the then-prominent Utah militia officer, Robert T. Burton. The Atkinson and McKinney families also operated a station across the river in these early years, all doubtless harvesting the natural hay abundant between the Upper and Lower Mojave Narrows. Even the station operators at Fishponds near future Daggett, the Lafeyette Mecham family, secured hay in this locality. Freighter Sheldon Stoddard eventually improved the road initially used to haul this hay by digging a well midway. This enabled other wagon drivers to save a full day's travel over the circuitous river route by taking the Stoddard's Well cut-off.

After 1872 the Victorville way station was operated by J.C. Farley and Thomas Kelly, the former recently of Pioche, Nevada. Farley brought with him a reputation for being disagreeable and by the following summer, the Kelly family was operating the business alone, although they had recently had dealings with Farley. In mid-August, the former partner drove up to the station constructed from picket-poles set vertically in the ground with a front fence four feet high built in the same manner. After Farley placed two bags of barley in his wagon, an argument arose over the price. When Kelly attempted to retrieve the grain, Farley drew his pistol and warned him to put it back. Kelly went into the house and secured his own gun. When he came back out his protagonist fired, with the bullet narrowly missing Kelly's wife, then standing in the doorway. The station operator shot back and killed a horse as both continued to fire at each other. Eventually Farley was hit in the upper thigh and ran away from the house still shooting. After seeing his opponent fall, Kelly went into the house for more ammunition. When there were no further shots, he took a horse to a nearby cattle camp to get a neutral party to investigate. Farley was discovered to have bled to death. Kelly gave himself up. With the testimony of witnesses that he was acting in self-defense, he was acquitted.

By 1874 Heber Huntington, born in Utah, had purchased the Victorville station and the one at Fish Ponds-Daggett and operated a station temporarily at Stoddard's Well. The newspapers were lavish in praising Huntington's wife for her "epicurean cuisine" and the establishment for its "accommodation and comfort" of the patrons. They operated the station for several years with good profits and satisfied customers. Several maps published during the decade designate the later Victorville vicinity as Huntington.

A 1917 illustration of the 1870s Huntington Station
History of Victor District,
San Bernardino County Archives

The greatest beneficiaries of the huge demand for food, merchandise and equipment in the high desert mining regions were the merchants of San Bernardino and elsewhere in the California southland, who promptly organized to fulfill the need. The Meyerstein firm obtained contracts from Panamint to Prescott, Arizona, to be delivered primarily by capable local freighters at good profits to all concerned. One county newspaperman smugly but accurately called the area "the granary and storehouse of the region." On one Saturday in 1873, 36 mining camp-bound wagon outfits were counted on one San Bernardino street.

Freight wagons outbound from San Bernardino for desert mining camps in boom era
Mohahve III

Cowboys gathering for valleywide rodeo roundup at Robinson Ranch near Helendale, c. 1890

Mohahve Historical Society

On a far smaller scale, the increasing number of residents along the Mojave River also profited considerably from the freighter traffic. Some Victor Valley ranchers shipped cattle to nearby mining camps as well as those in more distant Nevada and Arizona. Although the Mojave rangelands were still attractive to desperate outside cattlemen during the continuing southland droughts, by that time those more permanently occupying the vicinity were more successful resisting the trespasses of the outsiders.

The Bemis cabin, one of the first residences in Victor Valley, was built c.1873 and destroyed in the 1960s just before Silver Lake was developed.
Mohahve I

In early 1874 J.A. Rousseau and several other San Bernardino associates commenced surveys and preliminary land and water claims on lands in what would later be south Apple Valley. Calling their company the Valverde, a crew began digging canals to divert the Mojave flow to raise grain planted the ensuing year. The promoters asserted the vicinity was "highly adapted to the growth of cereals, vegetables and fruit... especially apples." Since there was no success in the venture, launched during a serious economic depression, its significance is in being the first of several concerted promotional schemes in the area.

One reason Aaron Lane remained so long in the vicinity was that he had found a piece of float or rich ore-bearing rock displaced from its original vein location in the hills. The vein was near his second ranch, which was located several miles downstream from his first homestead, later called Bryman. In February 1873 he brought rich ore to San Bernardino for assaying, which determined the sample to be "exceedingly rich," indicating location of the elusive vein. Although a few loads of ore were hauled down the Cajon, there is little evidence of extensive mine development. Soon thereafter, Lane sold his ranch to early Pomona residents named Phillips and Blake for $10,000.

By that time the first semblance of community in the area, initially called simply the Mojave River Settlement, was growing as a series of ranches situated on river bottomlands between Lane's Crossing and Point of Rocks. After Lane and his earlier neighbors, including the Edward Prothero family, who like Lane later resided at several river locations, the William Robinson and Bemis families arrived in the early 1870s. Long associated with cattle grazing and tragedy in the vicinity, Amos Bemis built a log cabin near Helendale in 1873. On several occasions later, the William Robinson family claimed first residence (after Lane) in local newspaper items and was not challenged in the assertion. Like many of their neighbors, they had originally been Mormon, but when leaving Utah, had apparently abandoned active affiliation with the church. This included the families of Ephraim D. Boren, William A. Downey and J.J. Davidson. Other early settlers on the considerable expanse of river bottoms with good agricultural potential were the families of George DeCrow of Iowa, James B. Bledsoe of Texas, J.D. Clark, Douglas Van Horn and Asa Lane, nephew of the original pioneer.

By 1880 there was already a school building in the settlement. Like others in the region thereafter, the building was doubtless an all-purpose community center housing Christmas parties, grange and club meetings, county elections and perhaps some religious services. Most families were self-sufficient as far as food was concerned. But San Bernardino-based merchant-peddlers were known to have made business visits in the area.

One of the problems common to all of the settlements north of Cajon Pass was the woeful lack of U.S mail service. Both the Mojave River residents and those of the mining camps depended on the semiregular freight wagon drivers to voluntarily bring the mail from the San Bernardino Post Office. In mid-1873 they petitioned California Congressman S.O. Houghton for better service, arguing

First schoolhouse in Victor Valley, c. early 1880s, on land donated by Aaron Lane at Bryman
Mohahve Historical Society

that citizens should not have to depend on voluntary service from facilities up to 150 miles away. The next year, former roadmaker Jed Van Dusen secured the contract to carry mail from San Bernardino to Prescott, Arizona. This was not a permanent solution for the citizens along the Mojave. Several years later the U.S. Postmaster General rerouted the service to the newly completed Southern Pacific Railroad station at Mojave in the Antelope Valley, thus bypassing the growing community.

Even more upsetting to many river settlers was the fact that they had to pay a toll every time they traveled through Cajon Pass. A letter to the editor of the San Bernardino *Guardian* in 1873 deplored this situation and called upon the county supervisors to rescind the franchise granted a dozen years before. The most consistent critic of the toll road and frequent evader of the fees was Capt. A.G. Lane. In 1875 he circulated a petition "numerously signed" arguing that the toll rates were "excessive" and requested that the old road be reopened as an alternative. The petitioners promised to maintain it at their own expense rather than submit to continuing the unfair situation. The next year, the San Bernardino *Times-Index* editorialized about the many complaints from Mojave River residents and the possibility that they might legitimately express their disgust toward the county seat by diverting their trade to the Antelope Valley to the west. The editor called for the road to be maintained at public expense, with the remaining years of the old toll franchise purchased at a fair price. It is clear no such action was taken on the matter before completion of the railroad a decade later.

Schoolgirl Marie Osborne's sketch of what she identified as Sam Rogers' 1870s ranch structure across the Mojave River from later downtown Victorville
History of Victor District
San Bernardino County Archives

One of the most important early residents in the vicinity between the upper and lower narrows of the Mojave River was Samuel Rogers, who emigrated to California during the first year of the gold rush. Later he followed the similar rush to Holcomb Valley, where he acquired part interest in a mine he retained for many years. In the late 1870s he commenced purchasing real estate and possessory claims, including the "Old Huntington Stage Station," eventually paying $1,500 for that property. By then this included station buildings on both sides of the river, along with some outlying structures and an adobe house and stable located just over a mile downstream on lands Rogers acquired by squatters' rights.

In 1876 Rogers began developing an extensive irrigation system, taking water from the Mojave just below the Upper Narrows by use of a brush and rock dam and an intake ditch. Utilizing existing sloughs, he dug a ditch along the contours of the bluffs on the south and west side of the river conveying water for more than a mile through the area, which a decade later would be the center of Victorville. He did not have clear title to all of the property crossed, which would eventually lead to lawsuits. But for many years water was effectively delivered to his homestead, where he planted barley and later claimed to be the first in the area to raise alfalfa.

For reasons some have asserted to include laziness, Rogers frequently engaged tenant farmers to do the actual work of operating his ranch. His brother William was thus engaged, along with early valley residents Heronymous Hartman and Lowery Silver. Rogers had quarrels with all of these men, leading to legal action to resolve the conflicts with the latter two. In the fall of 1879 he evicted Silver, undoubtedly when he learned his tenant was attempting to acquire part of the property through the Los Angeles Federal Land Office. Hartman's case was similar. He claimed Rogers agreed to grant him one-third interest in the proceeds of the crops raised, but the owner reneged on the contract. At some point Hartman attempted to gain legal title to some of Rogers' property, which probably caused the latter to cancel their agreements.

Bitterness over these matters undoubtedly led to the far more serious conflict featuring an exchange of gunfire. It appeared that Rogers was fencing across an old road no longer in use when Hartman approached by wagon with a pistol visible in his hand. This was clearly a culminating episode in a long-standing dispute that included recent threats. When the wagon was still some 30 or more yards distant, Rogers fired a shotgun loaded with buckshot. Hartman retaliated with a shot from his pistol that forced the landowner to retreat for his own

Wing dam diverting irrigation water from Upper Mojave Narrows River channel for Samuel Rogers' ditch
Victor Valley Museum and Art Gallery

The first photograph of what soon became downtown Victor, taken in the mid-1880s (just as the railroad company was establishing the town) shows Rogers' ditch running parallel to the river toward a ranch.
Victor Valley Museum and Art Gallery

Oro Grande Mine some years after its heyday
Mohahve I

an ore sample that proved to be almost solid silver. "Considerable excitement" brought prospectors from throughout the region to an area soon named Oro Grande. The post office opened at the town that quickly sprang up and was initially named Halleck, probably after one of the investors who bought the original mining location. Within six months the town bustled with miners, many still camped among the cottonwood trees while others built houses. Ed Johnson had already established a general store and two others opened butcher shops. A boarding house and hotel were also in operation.

The new mine owners soon filed on Mojave River water with the intention of establishing an ore reduction mill. The company purchased a water-powered, 10-stamp mill aiming to process the fine gold as well as silver being drawn from a cluster of mines situated in the low mountains about six miles north of Oro Grande, also the name for a leading mine. Area freight wagon proprietor J.D. Burkhart hauled up to 25 tons of ore per day. Within a year, the proprietors added a melting furnace in an attempt to more effectively process difficult ores.

Initially, the miners at Halleck-Oro Grande were mainly Chinese, supervised by whites. However, during an era of great prejudice against the Asians, conflicts arose, supposedly relating to refusal to follow directions. The subsequent firing of the Chinese may have been desired since they had to be aware of countrymen making more money helping construct a railroad from San Diego through Cajon Pass.

A short time after the beginnings of Oro Grande, a much larger camp commenced booming about 40 miles north at Calico. Since water was less available in that vicinity, operators of some of the most productive mines contracted with the Oro Grande company to have their ore reduced. The ore was hauled in wagons carrying 12 tons, each pulled by 18 good horses and mules. The railroad would replace this phase of the operation within a couple of years.

safety. Hartman was arrested and taken to jail at San Bernardino, where, because he could not raise bail, he spent considerable time. The trial was frequently postponed partly due to the difficulty of bringing the requisite witnesses to the county seat.

The Hartman Case was still undecided the next spring when other river valley residents named Snoderly and Henry Fulton engaged in a similar altercation, with the former shot in the shoulder and Fulton convicted of assault with intent to commit murder.

The attempts to settle disputes through violence were but the main evidence the area was still in the beginnings of frontier development experiencing problems typical of that process throughout the history of the nation. It was seemingly a part of the stage preceding maturity, which was about to arrive.

After years of rumors of the presence of rich ore deposits in the vicinity, in May 1880 A.J. Spencer, a partner of Aaron Lane, who had never profited much from his own discoveries, arrived at San Bernardino with

Rock-laden wagon used in Oro Grande area

The Kingdom of the Sun, Mohahve Historical Society

3 CHAPTER THREE 1880-1910

Ushering Victor Valley into the Modern World

(Opening photo)
Pictured is the railroad bridge just northwest of Victor before it was double- tracked. Supported by huge granite abutments, it is the oldest structure in Victor Valley, dating from 1884.
Mohahve I

The development that did most to assure the continued growth of the high desert was the building of a railroad through its southern segment. Early surveyors determined that the Cajon Pass must be utilized as an entrance to the California southland from the northeast, and they were virtually certain a tunnel through the summit ridge was necessary. Sen. John P. Jones of Nevada commenced such a project in the early 1870s, but economic depression and rivalry from the Southern Pacific Railroad forced him to abandon it. In November 1879 San Bernardino County Surveyor Frederick T. Perris journeyed to San Diego to persuade Boston railroad builders to consider Cajon Pass as an entrance to the San Diego Bay area. In this he succeeded, also convincing the locating engineers of the feasibility of a reasonable railroad grade through the east wing of the Cajon Pass. By making a considerable cut through the top ridge, a railroad could be built even without a tunnel.

Beginning in National City just south of San Diego, the California Southern Railroad, a subsidiary of the Atchison, Topeka & Santa Fe Railway Company, constructed a line northward toward the San Bernardino area, with Perris supervising much of the project. In 1882 he brought Chinese construction crews into the Cajon Pass area to begin grading. He also led in locating the most suitable grade from the summit to junction with the Atlantic & Pacific-Santa Fe line at Waterman, soon named Barstow. Two years later, after heavy Mojave River flooding, he altered the route slightly by eliminating one of the two bridges planned for the river, thus keeping the railroad mainly east of the river.

Perris' direct superior, a longtime railroad builder and an expert on trestles, Jacob Nash Victor of Ohio was fully involved in planning the bridge across the Mojave. The huge granite abutment, the oldest structure in the Victor Valley, is still in use. The other great feats of this project were the massive cut at the top of the Cajon summit, and the rainwater diversion chutes to prevent mud slides in the same area. Another feature of the new railroad was a "Y" track for turning around locomotive engines, designated as "Victor helpers," which assisted heavily loaded freight trains up the grade toward the Cajon summit. One of these was just below the summit cut and the other 15 miles down the track where the town of Victor soon came into existence. The railroad also designated Victor as the location for its station, telegraph office and water tank, much to the displeasure of already-established Oro Grande. Completion of the railroad near the end of 1885 not only broke Southern Pacific Railroad's monopoly on overland transportation into Southern California but stimulated a passenger rate war that brought a huge influx of Easterners into the state.

Building the California Southern-Santa Fe Railroad through Cajon Pass, Chinese workmen made the crucial cut through the summit, a heroic feat of labor in 1884.
Photo by Fred T. Perris, Steele's Photo Service
Victor Valley College Library Local History Collection

The coming of the railroad also stimulated mining and ushered in new granite and marble quarrying industries in both Oro Grande and infant Victor. Some promoters in the area boasted their marble to be equal to the best in Italy. Entrepreneurs transformed the old Oro Grande mill into one for finishing the stone for shipment. In 1887 other foresiteful businessmen recognized the limestone in several local mountains to be excellent for manufacturing cement. Within a year at least four small kilns were erected for that purpose, ushering in Victor Valley's chief industry for the next century. Some limestone was also shipped for use in silver reduction processing near Calico, and for beet sugar refining in Chino and elsewhere.

From the time the railroad arrived, Oro Grande area boosters had lauded their desert climate as perfect for the kind of health resorts just beginning to flourish in the entire region. The San Bernardino *Courier* editor testified the high desert climate had cured him of catarrh troubles, and several San Bernardino physicians prescribed Oro Grande as the "best resort of hope to patients suffering from any form of pulmonary disease." Robert Turner was informed by Colton Dr. W. E. Fox that his two older children would soon die if the family did not move to the desert. The Turners soon built a two-story house at Adelanto Springs, near Oro Grande and close to the historic Lane's Crossing. Mrs. Turner operated the home partly as a health resort for several years. Though slighted by the railroad, Oro Grande continued to flourish, erecting a substantial second school building in 1890, which still stands as a church.

In number of businesses, if not permanent population, Victor surpassed Oro Grande by mid-1888. The

"Y" track arrangement for turning around "Victor helper" locomotives at the Cajon summit after they have assisted heavy freight trains up the grade from Victorville
Photo by Fred T. Perris, Steele's Photo Service
Mohahve Historical Society

(Far right)
One of American Beet Sugar Company's mule teams transporting lime rock from quarries to railway cars for shipment to Chino and Oxnard factories
The Kingdom of the Sun

P. J. Fleming pot kiln remnants still on Oro Grande cement plant property many years after the industry was started there
Mohahve I

(Far right)
Mule team at the bottom of a huge limestone quarry in Oro Grande before 1900
Huntington Library, Art Collections & Botanical Gardens

The Morrow brothers and others seated on the bank of the Mojave River near Oro Grande, probably during a summer holiday celebration in the 1890s
Mojave River Valley Museum, Barstow, donated by Penny Morrow

Chilson family opened a good hotel, and the Turners later moved from their ranch to build several businesses in the new town, including a hotel and a restaurant. The livery stable and blacksmith shop were busy from the beginning. At that time the general store was operated by I. D. Parish. The county board of supervisors broke off a Victor School District from Oro Grande and it soon created a makeshift elementary school. In contrast to the rival town, Victor began as a "temperance town, no saloons allowed."

Like those in Oro Grande, Victor residents quarried marble and limestone, but soon engaged more particularly in granite blocks of various sizes, then much in demand for buildings and city streets. Victor granite orders went to Los Angeles and San Francisco for both purposes. These industries depended on the railroad, which also stimulated a growing amount of freight and stage transport from Victor to the far-flung mining camps.

The most famous land rush in Southern California history peaked in 1888. The frenzy for real estate profits, a longtime preoccupation in Victor Valley, actually commenced near Victor in 1887. As usual, government lands were available for private entry by citizens, but many depended on guidance from "locators" supposedly more familiar with the area and entry procedures. Outspoken *Courier* editor Arthur Kearney warned that most good land had already been claimed, perhaps hoping to sell his own holdings north of Oro Grande. According to the newspaperman, "tenderfoots" were reportedly entering on lands he considered "utterly valueless" desert. Still another reporter asserted "the whole country between the Mojave River and Rabbit Springs Lucerne Valley was

(Far left)
Pictured is the end of the four-mile ditch that was cut into the side of Deep Creek Canyon to convey Hesperia Land and Water Company water. From this point water entered a hand-riveted siphon pipe that went under the Mojave River channel and up onto the far Hesperia mesa for the new settlers.
Victor Valley Museum and Art Gallery

End of Deep Creek aqueduct near Lime Street Park, Hesperia
San Bernardino County Museum

alive with surveyors and the men and parties hunting land." Another reported the "desert full of men" traveling by stage load, carrying maps and locating land. One of the factors encouraging promoters to continue the boom was the success of some new homesteaders. Edward Dolch, who left the Germanys to avoid induction into the army, took up a homestead far from water in 1887 and successfully began growing fruit trees without irrigation. These did not survive a second year as the usual dry weather conditions resumed, but in the meantime his ranch served as a showplace of what could be accomplished.

The other community born partly as a result of the completion of the railroad was Hesperia. In 1888, Robert M. Widney, a longtime Southern California real estate promoter, revealed his ingenious plan for delivering water to the land his company had recently purchased. He brilliantly diverted Deep Creek water into a canal that was blasted out of the side of Deep Creek Canyon. The former Nevada mining engineer maintained sufficient elevation to utilize an inverted siphon fashioned from a 14-inch, hand-riveted pipe-culvert, which ran more than a mile through the Mojave River and up onto the Hesperia mesa lands. The aqueduct terminated at a distribution reservoir just west of the railroad tracks near future Lime Street Park.

Within days of completion of the water project, the Hesperia Company, capitalized at $4 million and backed by some of the leading bankers and businessmen of the Los Angeles area, commenced a concentrated real estate promotional campaign. This featured large ads in all three Los Angeles daily newspapers, stressing the healthful climate and promising agricultural possibilities. Some advertised round-trip excursions from downtown Los Angeles to Hesperia. Reporters who took that trip lauded customer treatment as well as the potential of the undertaking. Amidst Southern California's land boom of 1888 there were numerous other schemes competing for customer interests. But some people reportedly invested in Hesperia at that time — five homes appeared during the first weeks along with a hotel, general store and post office. The three-story, 50-bedroom hotel, which became the area's primary landmark, took two years to complete. The school was also completed in 1890.

The following year, former Michigan schoolteacher and Civil War veteran W.W. Poates purchased interest in a nearby sawmill and aimed to open a lumber yard. But before long tragedy struck when intermittent poor health and emotional lapses led Poates to take his own life. His widow would later found Apple Valley.

Although the land boom faded before Hesperia experienced much growth, a few families did establish apple and fig trees. Early in the 1890s grape vines produced a truly phenomenal series of raisin crops. Unfortunately, the well-conceived water system was not effective in time of flood or drought. Each prevented water delivery at least

Extensive raisin-drying operation in Hesperia in the 1890s
San Bernardino County Museum

As Victor continued to grow, the county board of supervisors approved the Upper Mojave Narrows as the location for the first major bridge over the river. Oro Grande citizens were furious about this, but even wagons hauling ore to their mills could better cross the Mojave near Victor. Unfortunately, the bridge contractor advocated a clearly flawed design for the structure. When railroad engineers and others demanded a test of the new bridge strength, it failed. With approximately half the townspeople watching in late September 1890, the bridge collapsed, dumping at least seven men, a mule team and a loaded ore wagon into the river 50 feet below. The next year the county contracted for a more substantial bridge at the same spot.

Victor remained the primary distribution point for several productive mines from Holcomb Valley northward into the desert. Larger establishments sent semirefined bullion for shipment abroad for future processing. However, smaller-claim holders could not afford their own reduction mills and hoped a local custom operation might make their mines profitable. In late 1897 the Boston and Fantasma Milling and Mining Company erected a 10-stamp mill near the Victor bridge, aiming to perform crushing work and perhaps processing for others, along with milling their own ores. Yet when the mill began operation, customers did not take advantage of the situation. This was partly because the extended economic depression caused precious metal prices to remain low. Just when the situation was about to turn around, the plant equipment was attached for debt and sold at auction, with the main mill works relocated to another area.

By the spring of 1897 there were just over 600 inhabitants in Victor. The town had three hotels, two stores,

one season in the decade, which proved fatal to most agricultural ventures at that time.

For some time, the main Hesperia economic endeavor was cutting the vast stands of juniper for firewood. The wood was shipped by railroad to Los Angeles. The extent of the enterprise may be gauged from the loss of 1,500 cords of wood, each 4 feet wide and high and 8 feet long, which burned at the wood storage square near the railroad depot at an estimated loss of $4,000. Just after 1900 and some conflict with federal government officials over cutting the junipers, the industry continued to flourish for a decade. The community was characterized by several other bitter quarrels as well, including one with the Hesperia Land and Water Company over culinary water rates.

Hesperia school built in 1890
Hesperia: A Pictorial History

several eating establishments and a Chinese laundry. Freight and livery services also continued to expand. And the town, having temporarily abandoned prohibition, also included a wholesale liquor store and at least one saloon. A Congregational minister, Rev. Case, organized a Sunday school at that time. Mr. Auchunachie, a longtime area justice of the peace, preached occasionally and held religious services every other Sunday at the schoolhouse. He also delivered most funeral sermons and performed most community marriages. There were frequent dances also held at the school and in new houses and stores before they were furnished.

With the success of tapping the Santa Ana River and other streams running south from the San Bernardino Mountains, there would soon be interest in similarly utilizing the waters of the Mojave River running northward. In February 1893 a Minnesota company secured options on existing water claims and the most logical dam-reservoir site above the Upper Mojave Narrows. Recent surveys determined that up to 250,000 acres of surrounding land could be irrigated with water retained behind a dam projected to be 170 feet high and up to 150 feet wide. Unfortunately, the so-called Panic of '93 thwarted progress by the original company. The next year another corporation, headquarted in Springfield, Illinois, took over the project and surveys with help from some of the earlier participants, but they too made little progress. Then in 1895 a third firm, the Columbia Colonization Company of Chicago, tried its hand. This company was headed by J.W. Wilson, publisher of *Field, Farm and Fireside*, a Midwestern farmers journal. Former Civil War and American Indian campaign veteran Gen. O.O. Howard was also involved. The new owners acquired the proposed Victor reservoir project for $80,000 and asserted it would be "the largest volume of water supplying an irrigation system in the world."

The Columbia Company claimed to have received more than 8,000 inquiries from people interested in relocating to Southern California. An appealing stipulation to some regarding the new colony, as in Riverside, Redlands and Ontario before it, was prohibition of the sale of alcoholic beverages within the project. In this land scheme, participants deeded back to the company 280 acres of the 320 acres entered under the Desert Land Act in exchange for sufficient water to irrigate their remaining 40 acres for a mere $80.00. As appealing as this proposition might have been to landless citizens, it is doubtful that the federal government would have approved of such an arrangement. As Gen. Howard subsequently withdrew from the venture, Wilson and several associates were discredited by negative newspaper reports of questionable dealings in another project at nearby Big Rock Creek in Antelope Valley. Additional complications arose when sellers in the second Victor reservoir company filed court suit to retrieve possession of the dam site and water rights because of failure of the Columbia Company to comply with the original purchase terms.

In the midst of Columbia Company promotions, a similar group of Los Angeles businessmen formed the Appleton Land and Water Company. Led by Judge P.D. Hatch of Los Angeles as president, it proposed to take water from the headwaters of the Mojave River and store it behind a dam some 12 miles above the already projected Victor Reservoir. This new company intended to convey water to lands east of Hesperia and Victor, said to be particularly well-adapted for alfalfa and deciduous fruit. Promoters claimed the fertile soil raised the finest apples in Southern California and for that reason derived the name Apple Valley for the new town. While the Appleton Company purchased several primary water rights on Mojave River tributaries, it sought to assure the neighboring companies there was no real rivalry since the Victor Reservoir aimed to store winter run-off water and the Appleton Company claimed summer season flows.

Even prior to companies organizing to tap the Mojave River for irrigation of the surrounding desert, the Arrowhead Reservoir Company was also organizing. It intended to utilize some of those same water supplies closer to the mountain sources and redirect them by tunnel through the San Bernardino Mountains to the more populous valleys to the south. The project was

Constructing the core wall of Little Bear or Lake Arrowhead dam around 1905

Photo by Steele's Photo Service, The San Bernardinos by John W. Robinson

conceived by longtime San Bernardino railroad engineer Fred T. Perris and passed on to fellow civil engineer A.H. Koebig, also involved in the Columbia Company. He located interested capitalists, particularly a group from Cincinnati, Ohio, including Gamble of the Proctor and Gamble Company.

The rivalries among these claimants of Mojave River water became even more concerted after the U.S. government dispatched surveyors to the area to ascertain the feasibility of the area as a dam and reservoir site. At the same time in 1899, Gifford Pinchot, head of the U.S.Bureau of Forestry, visited the area, which soon led to a detailed field study of the Mojave River watershed. In 1902 President Theodore Roosevelt and other advocates of reclamation of western arid lands finally secured the Newlands Act. Hopes arose in California, as in surrounding states, that the federal government might purchase available reservoir sites from private companies.

Later in the year, the inevitable legal battles between the Arrowhead Reservoir Company and other water interests along the Mojave River commenced. W.A. Field, president of the oldest corporate claimant of river water rights, the Hesperia Land and Water Company, filed protests that the defendant company was preparing to halt the natural flow of Deep Creek, Little Bear Valley Creek and other streams into the Mojave. He questioned its intent to divert the water toward an entirely different destination, through the mountains and down the southerly slopes to the San Bernardino Valley instead of northward on its natural course. The Arrowhead Company replied it was only interested in storm run-off waters virtually wasted during the previous dozen years. Its employees had been gauging such runoff. The Arrowhead Company went doggedly ahead with its large dam construction project, featuring a concrete core wall covered by a massive volume of landfill.

The logical means of eliminating downstream opposition was to purchase the water rights in that section. Throughout 1905 another syndicate represented by Arthur E. Poole of Los Angeles labored feverishly to accomplish that purpose. By the end of the year it held options on almost all of the lower Mojave River ranches and water rights. The old Brown-Verde Ranch, then owned by E.C. Sterling, was the biggest purchase at a reported cost of $335,000 for 4,000 acres. This was particularly crucial because it included the actual dam and reservoir sites on the property. At about the same time the syndicate purchased all remaining interests of the old Columbia Colonization Company in the area. Poole was careful not to reveal the firm he represented or what it intended to do with the Mojave water. Speculators conjectured that the water might be conveyed toward Los Angeles. The agent's brother, Charles O. Poole, was employed as one of the key engineers providing Los Angeles with all the water it would need for years of growth. Water was taken from the Owens River Valley residents, first covertly and eventually by aqueduct.

In early 1906 it was finally determined that Poole was backed by James Westwater, an Ohio financier. His company soon announced plans to immediately develop not only an irrigation project but also an electric power generation plant. By March the Westwater people had demonstrated the ability to carry out the project, and all former opposition appeared to be overcome. A contract was let to a Pittsburgh, Pennsylvania, company that had recently constructed a reservoir near Columbus, Ohio, for work on the Victorville dam to commence that summer. However, as many times before, financial difficulties intervened, preventing building of the dam. This time the San Francisco earthquake reportedly shattered the faith of Eastern capitalists who had agreed to assist with the project. After that James Westwater's financial empire appeared to crumble as well. California associates, including Poole, desperately fought to retain control of the Brown-Verde Ranch through securing additional loans and making payments to delay Sterling interests from resuming ownership. These efforts eventually failed.

Meantime, the Arrowhead Reservoir Company continued to maintain its Mojave water claims, renewing them every 60 days. When the San Bernardino *Sun* reported such actions in late August 1906, it led to a verbal outburst by W.A. Field, president of Hesperia

Lark Hotel, Victorville Harness Shop, and the Cottage Lunch eatery east of the railroad tracks
Mohahve I

Victorville Railroad Depot when it was situated on the east side of the tracks, with part of the earliest business section of town visible along E Street
Mohahve I

Land and Water Company, which was itself undoubtedly reinvigorated by the failure of Westwater interests. Field took strong exception to reports that implied the Arrowhead Company had secured control of all Mojave River water rights. He claimed the Hesperia company owned and controlled 33,000 acres of land bordering the Mojave and had filed on 1 million miners inches on both forks of the river two years prior to the earliest Arrowhead Company filings. In addition, Field asserted his company had utilized 5,000 inches of East Fork water each of the last 20 years. The company was adamant that no waters naturally draining into the Mojave would ever be diverted toward the San Bernardino Valley.

In 1909 other lawsuits were filed by Mojave River riparian owners against the Arrowhead Reservoir and Power Company to prevent the company from diverting water from the natural drainage region. Although the company had begun to purchase some down-river property to help alleviate opposition, the plans were halted. A decision in a San Joaquin Valley case before the state Supreme Court prohibited floodwaters from being diverted from their natural drainage area for agricultural purposes. This was undoubtedly devastating to the Arrowhead Company, which had already expended millions of dollars with ultimate plans to sell its water mainly in the San Bernardino Valley area. The existence of the lake and company depended on water that was naturally a part of the Mojave River water system. Therefore, the Supreme Court decision would help protect basin water users from further incursions on their resources, although it did not prohibit diversion for culinary use.

At the turn of the 20th century, the merchants of Victor, soon to be named Victorville through pressure from the U.S. Postal Service to eliminate similarity with Victor, Colorado, were busier and more prosperous than ever before. There were no idle workers in the town. At that time the business district, including a new railroad depot completed in 1907, was almost exclusively located north and east of the Santa Fe tracks. The original Parish general store, operated by a variety of managers, always featured a complete stock of equipment for miners and prospectors. The Richardson brothers, who had been engaged in area freighting for a decade, purchased the establishment in 1905. Robert and Susan Turner, residents of the old Lane's Crossing ranch for half a decade, seized the opportunity to grow with the burgeoning town of Victor. They purchased a block of land between 6th and 7th streets and C and D streets, where they built a two-story frame Turner House, long famous along the railroad line for good meals and clean beds. They also opened a general merchandise store on the business side of the tracks, although it was moved into a larger, new concrete building on the hotel side in 1902. This started a gradual shift of businesses across to the west side, which continued for a decade.

A significant historic photograph, taken early in the 1900s from the second story of the Turner House, reveals virtually no other structures between 6th and 8th streets

Redlands excursionists parked their Model-T Fords in front of the Turner Store, 1909.
Fun with Fritz
complied by William G. Moore

and the railroad tracks. The primary landowner, Appleton Land and Water Company, had cleared the land of cottonwood trees and undergrowth. The series of ponds and sloughs prevalent along the foot of the bluff extending east and west were filled because they were suspected of being health hazards. When the land company began laying out the streets, it logically conformed to the railroad line and the hilly terrain more than to the points of the compass. As homesteading activity accelerated late in the decade, the housing shortage became severe in Victorville as elsewhere in the valley. Several businessmen in town assisted in alleviating the problem by generating a building boom of their own. More residences were cropping up on the west side of the railroad tracks. That is also where the schools were established. There must have been an earlier one on the east side, although no known reference has yet been found.

In the summer of 1908 the Victorville School Board sold bonds worth $2,500 to finance a two-room addition, making a total of four, in the grade school located near 6th and C streets. That year the county school census indicated 79 Victorville students, which was up from 55 the year before. There were eight graduates who successfully passed the rigorous eighth-grade county exams. Since there was no high school in the desert, the older students who chose to continue their education boarded in San Bernardino or the Los Angeles area.

Under a series of owners, the Brown-Verde Ranch proved important because of the variety of economic endeavors pursued there. Sterling's British son-in-law, Reginald Frost, operated a dairy with a considerable herd of Jersey cows. Cattle ranching was always a primary undertaking, with hands like colorful Blue Thorpe and Tex Rankin heading a large crew of employees. There were also apple orchards, sugar beet crops, honeybee hives

The view from the second floor of the new Turner building on D Street shows no development in what would soon be the main business section of Victor. The business district of E Street is partly visible beyond the railroad tracks, c. 1902.
Victor Valley College Library Local History Collection

Redlands excursionists parked their Model-T Fords in front of the Turner Store, 1909.
Fun with Fritz
compiled by William G. Moore

and the railroad tracks. The primary landowner, Appleton Land and Water Company, had cleared the land of cottonwood trees and undergrowth. The series of ponds and sloughs prevalent along the foot of the bluff extending east and west were filled because they were suspected of being health hazards. When the land company began laying out the streets, it logically conformed to the railroad line and the hilly terrain more than to the points of the compass. As homesteading activity accelerated late in the decade, the housing shortage became severe in Victorville as elsewhere in the valley. Several businessmen in town assisted in alleviating the problem by generating a building boom of their own. More residences were cropping up on the west side of the railroad tracks. That is also where the schools were established. There must have been an earlier one on the east side, although no known reference has yet been found.

In the summer of 1908 the Victorville School Board sold bonds worth $2,500 to finance a two-room addition, making a total of four, in the grade school located near 6th and C streets. That year the county school census indicated 79 Victorville students, which was up from 55 the year before. There were eight graduates who successfully passed the rigorous eighth-grade county exams. Since there was no high school in the desert, the older students who chose to continue their education boarded in San Bernardino or the Los Angeles area.

Under a series of owners, the Brown-Verde Ranch proved important because of the variety of economic endeavors pursued there. Sterling's British son-in-law, Reginald Frost, operated a dairy with a considerable herd of Jersey cows. Cattle ranching was always a primary undertaking, with hands like colorful Blue Thorpe and Tex Rankin heading a large crew of employees. There were also apple orchards, sugar beet crops, honeybee hives

The view from the second floor of the new Turner building on D Street shows no development in what would soon be the main business section of Victor.
The business district of E Street is partly visible beyond the railroad tracks, c. 1902.
Victor Valley College Library Local History Collection

The hall had been built two years previously. Some of the ladies of Victorville, including Mrs. Cochrane and Mrs. John Talmadge, began raising money for a new town hall. They formed a small stock company, selling some shares, along with soliciting funds from local businessmen. The women also held socials, dinners and dances. By the end of the year the last social event was held in the old Turner hall, presumably the largest room in the hotel. The new Victorville Hall was a 30-foot-wide, 60-foot-long structure built for dances and social gatherings, including hosting the small theatrical groups that occasionally passed through the town. On at least one later occasion the building was called the Stock Company Hall. The building stood east of the railroad tracks and was later used as a church by some of the local African-American residents.

For more than 60 years into the 20th century, the "city dads," mainly members of the chamber of commerce, were simply interested citizens who functioned in place of local government officials. They lobbied with county administration for improvements the community needed. Sometimes they focused their townsmen's attention on projects that needed to be accomplished. One of the most important was organizing a volunteer fire department. It was equipped with a little red hose cart pulled and pushed by firemen racing into action. The "fire call" usually came from a Victor "helper locomotive whistle."

The first town of Victor Valley, Oro Grande, remained a bustling and prosperous community. Besides the extensive mining and quarrying, perhaps the most important endeavor developing the major industry of the region for the next century, cement manufacturing, was taking place. In the spring of 1908, the lime burning enterprise, which had existed in the area for two decades, began to mushroom. The Golden State Portland Cement Company, initially comprised mainly of Los Angeles capitalists, announced plans for a plant that would produce 2,500 barrels of cement per day. The link to the former lime kiln operations was F.O. Wyman, the first to engage in lime burning in the area, who undoubtedly apprised others of the high quality and immense volume of the essential limestone deposits in the vicinity. A type of clay essential to the process was also located within 25 miles. First notice of company intentions placed W.P. Echdahl, former manager of a cement plant in South Chicago, in charge of the new California facility, with W.A. Potts serving as secretary.

Mrs. E.M. Potts, business manager and leading promoter of the Golden State Portland Cement Company
The Kingdom of the Sun

Within a short time the wife of the secretary emerged as a prime mover in the entire company operation. Mrs. Potts, reared in luxury in an English home, came to America as a bride and lived most of her adult life in Southern California. As family interest grew in the cement industry, W.A. Potts, an experienced architect, visited some of the best-designed plants in the country before planning and supervising the construction of the Oro Grande facility. At some point Mrs. Potts sought some of the necessary capital among her girlhood friends in England. With a combination of infectious enthusiasm and the tenacity of a bulldog, she not only generated much of the financial backing but, as business manager, also continued to oversee much of the administration of the company throughout the initial years. By July 1910 the main plant building, described as a "most imposing structure," neared completion. In October the giant kiln arrived and was set in place. The next month a test run determined the machinery to be in excellent working condition, as was the electric power generating facility to be

Golden State Portland Cement Company plant as it looked in its first years
The Kingdom of the Sun

utilized until later connection with outside power sources. Observers commented that every company undertaking was of the highest quality and workmanship.

Probably aware that a scarcely veiled antagonism existed in Oro Grande when the cement plant was being constructed, Mrs. Potts staged several special events recognizing key mileposts of the local company endeavor. The most important of these took place in late November 1910, when the Golden State Portland Cement Company hosted a dance and reception in recognition of the plant commencing to crush rock and make clinker — even if it was not quite ready to grind the final cement product in the incomplete finishing mill. Mrs. Potts was called on to formally announce the starting of the plant. With proper ceremony, she turned on the electric lights in the town hall for the first time. The town hall was one of the several buildings to which the company offered newly available self-generated electric power.

A kiln installed inside the original Golden State Portland Cement plant
The Kingdom of the Sun

A contemporary observer wrote in the local promotional magazine, *The Kingdom of the Sun*, that such events generated hearty cooperation and good will toward the company, particularly the business manager. Mrs. Potts usually resided and worked in Los Angeles, while her husband and sometimes a son and daughter lived in Oro Grande, where she was a frequent visitor. When company and community members heard that "Madam" was coming, there was a general cleanup of the premises to please her. At about the time the main cement works were completed, one San Bernardino newspaprman knowingly concluded, "Mrs. E.M. Potts, business manager of the plant, deserves a great deal of praise for the ingenuity which she has displayed in bringing this to completion with success." This impressive lady demonstrated her greatest abilities and accomplishments even before California women gained the right to vote.

Shown is one of eight large quarries in the mountains near Oro Grande. The photo included possible English investors in the cement plant, attracted by Mrs. E.M. Potts.
The Kingdom of the Sun

Except for temporary shutdowns for essential materials such as fuel oil and gypsum, the plant ran at full capacity, two shifts per day, with the night crew enjoying electric lighting throughout the entire premises. Newspaper observers noted that the company, even during the construction stage, intended to soon dispense with most of the unskilled labor in order to attract "more competent," and perhaps more reliable workers who had families. The company had erected cottages for families from the beginning, but in the development phase it also built boarding house facilities, presumably for single men, at both the quarry and the cement plant. More family housing would be added later. Prior to the plant commencing work, the company employed a Chicago physician, first headquartered in a tent, to provide medical care. Midway in the building process, Mr. Potts purchased the Oro Grande general store, with the understanding that the cement company would eventually purchase it from him. The selection of merchandise thereafter improved markedly to the appreciation of all. Thus Oro Grande had some of the trappings of an early 20th-century company town, common in the era, although not in Southern California.

One of Golden State Portland Cement Company's early rock trains used to transport lime rock from quarries to the Oro Grande cement plant
The Kingdom of the Sun

4 CHAPTER FOUR 1900-1925

Attempting to Build an Agricultural Empire

(Opening photo)
Bell Mountain School between 1910 and 1920 — (from left) Miss Keep, teacher, and Ruby Cook; (from right) Mrs. Stanley, superintendent of schools, and Joseph Cook
Mohahve Historical Society

One of the questions relating to the history of Victor Valley in the early 20th century is why, after a decade of relative quiescence, the interest in homesteading again climbed toward a peak in the first two decades after 1900. And similarly, since the majority of the ventures ultimately failed and the people abandoned the area, why was there so much pride in the reminiscences of the process of taking the desert land and trying, albeit unsuccessfully, to make a living from it? In the earlier years of U.S. history, the free and cheap land on the Western frontier had served as an effective magnet attracting venturesome individuals from areas where they had no prospects of ever being landowners. After the longest economic depression yet experienced in the nation began to subside just prior to the 20th century, a renewed interest in taking up new farmland appeared. More public land was claimed in the 20 years after 1900 than in the 40 years prior to that date.

This was partly stimulated by the rapid increase in the value of farmland during the years after 1890, along with the related price increases of farm commodities. Equally important were the laws Congress passed and amended, making the remaining public lands more easily obtainable. The original Homestead Act of 1862 allowed ownership of 160 acres providing the claimants resided on the premises for three years. This could actually be shortened to 14 months' residence through the payment of a fee of $1.25 per acre. The Desert Land Act of 1891 stipulated that if the land so entered was irrigated and producing within three years, it could be permanently patented at that time. And even more attractive, in 1909 the Enlarged Homestead Act was finally passed, which allowed claimants 320 acres of land without having to irrigate it. However, they did need to bring one-eighth of the acreage into cultivation within three years, and it required five years' residence on the land to gain final title.

The eased requirements of the 1909 law can be traced to President Theodore Roosevelt. In 1908 he appointed a Commission on Country Life comprised of men committed to publicize farming as a "dignified and virtuous way of making a living and that ordinarily it was the environment best suited to the raising of responsible and well-adjusted children." The country life movement was gradually transformed into the back-to-the-land movement, which naturally spawned liberalization of the national homesteading policy. Also influential was a new and highly specialized type of agriculture known as dry land farming that had recently shown promise of transforming previously unusable lands into productive agricultural districts. Besides utilizing drought-resistant crops, this featured proper cultivating of the soil to retain all available moisture and allowing the land to lay fallow every other year so that two years of precipitation were held on any particular field to mature a crop.

Most of the earliest homesteading of this time centered along the Mojave River in what was becoming known as Apple Valley. When the Appleton Land and Water Company first appeared and expressed intent to promote land development in the area, officials asserted it grew the "finest apples of any section in the southern part of the state." It is not now known that any homestead was established or that anyone was in the process of producing apples at the time of this statement in 1895. It is evident, however, that some homestead entries were made in the 1870s and that Ursula Poates began taking up land there in 1890.

Ursula M. Poates, the real pioneer and chief early promoter of Apple Valley
The Kingdom of the Sun

While many of the historical details are still obscure, it is clear that the real founder of Apple Valley, and reportedly the first to use that name, was Ursula M. Poates. Formerly of Hesperia, she was fondly called the "Mayoress of Apple Valley" in 1911. Later accounts attest to Poates as the first semipermanent resident of Apple Valley. She was clearly credited with being the area's "most energetic booster." As the San Bernardino *Sun* observed, she "controlled thousands of acres in the valley and [had] been the means of attracting hundreds of homesteaders to the zone of her operations." The 1911 newspaper article continued, "through the personal efforts of Mrs. Poates hundreds of acres of Apple Valley have been transformed into orchards and grain fields, while the waters underlying the valley have been tapped and the valley placed on an independent footing in many instances for irrigation water." Or so it seemed.

The next residents of Apple Valley in 1902 started locating on the first mesa of raised land adjacent the Mojave River, west of later Apple Valley Road and both sides of future Bear Valley Road. Some claimed ranches farther north, closer to the main bridge and the eventual Highway 18. A few came from the Los Angeles area by wagon and some brought all their furniture and equipment by "pioneer car" boxcar to the Hesperia or Victorville railroad sidings. Many resided in tents and lean-tos until more substantial houses were completed. Rabbits and coyotes presented major problems, partly solved with special net fencing material. Birds could not be kept out of the hay and grain fields so easily. Some planted apple and other fruit trees early in the homesteading process, although there were no reports of commercial fruit sales in these first years.

Several early settlers diverted river water onto their fields, but quickly concluded the river did not flow with sufficient regularity for direct irrigation purposes. Harry Cardon had been advised by a local well-driller to file on land close to the Mojave River, possibly because it was clear the water table was higher there, good advice for all who could find such unclaimed property. Some dug wells by hand and installed windmills to provide culinary water, hauling it by wagon from the Verde Ranch until their own water facilities were completed. Most employed one of the several well drillers to develop larger water sources, installing pumping equipment propelled by stationary distillate-propelled engines. Eventually earth-banked storage reservoirs retained the water pumped through the night and distributed during the day to orchard trees and other crops through small concrete pipes.

George B. Holbrook irrigating an apple tree in northern Apple Valley in the summer of 1913
Mohahve Historical Society, Allen Fletcher Collection

The John Carroll ranch proved particularly significant because it was the site of the first school in the Apple Valley district in 1908. The law stipulated six students were required to receive public funds. Since there were yet but five eligible children in the area, the enterprising Carroll recruited Esther Larson, perhaps a relative, from Long Beach. She, along with Irene and Jack Carroll, Edith and Wilma Foster, and Bill Phillips were taught that year by Clara Maurer. Later the far northern portion of the Westphal ranch on Bear Valley at Deep Creek Road was donated for use as a new school site. The contract for building this school was let in the summer of 1909. Since Clara Maurer was still the teacher for the 1910 school year and hosted an Apple Valley Country Club social at the school that spring, she and her class probably finished that school year in the new building. The Apple Valley Social Club used the building some evenings and infrequent "preaching services" were held whenever a visiting minister was available. Sunday school was more regular from the beginning. Christmas programs featuring the school children were also staged at the school. "Splendid" Independence Day celebrations were often held under the cooling cottonwood trees near the excellent swimming holes along the Mojave River.

(Far right)
Stone house completed in late 1910 on a homestead near Bell Mountain while builder Bronson recorded aspects of his life in an extant diary
Mohahve Historical Society, Bronson Collection

Apple Valley School built in 1910 at Bear Valley and Deep Creek roads
Mohahve I

Homesteading activity in Victor Valley accelerated after pronouncements from President Roosevelt and passage of the enlarged Homestead Act of 1909. The transcontinental railroads, including the Santa Fe, offered lower transportation rates from the East and Midwest. For a time thousands came to California every day to locate on new farmlands. The often-used Desert Land Act stipulated that 20 acres be brought into cultivation each of the second and third years. Fruit trees fit this requirement better than field crops because water to irrigate the trees could be carried by bucket until the more complex water systems were completed.

Early 1900s Independence Day picnic and rodeo near Mojave River
Hesperia: A Pictorial History

The lower Mojave River area below Oro Grande also attracted early homesteaders, largely because several long-time residents of the first section settled in the valley had enjoyed bumper fruit crops. In 1910, while area fruit crops were bending tree branches, a private railroad car stopped at the Oro Grande sidetrack and 40 landseekers took previously arranged teams and wheeled conveyances into the desert in search of lands to file on. The group returned to have dinner in the railroad car and spent the remainder of the evening playing cards. The hotel was filled to overflowing, with many guests lodging for the night at local homes. The accompanying newspaper reporter understated the situation when he said the "Mojave Desert in general [was] becoming a source of much attraction to home seekers."

Well-drilling rig used to procure water for early Victor Valley ranches
The Kingdom of the Sun

Between 1910 and 1920 all indications were that Victor Valley was about to emerge as one of the premier agricultural regions in Southern California. Several newspaper reports that had stated almost every section of land had been claimed in an area about 50 miles square were undoubtedly exaggerations, but there was indeed a phenomenal number of land entries. The valley population was little more than a thousand in the 1910 census but quite possibly more than doubled that within a half-dozen years. There is no way to carefully enumerate the number of "traction engines" (soon to be named tractors), gang plows, drags and other land-leveling equipment in use at the time, but every newspaper column written about the valley during the era mentions more land being developed.

While the traditional grain and alfalfa crops were frequently interspersed, it was deciduous fruit production on which the rampant optimism was based. There were many reports of 40-acre orchards planted and several with thousands of acres and 10,000 trees, and plans for more. One Utah nurseryman claimed to have delivered five railroad carloads of sapling fruit trees with others coming from Oregon and Missouri and points in between.

By the fall of 1912 there were 12 well-drilling companies in operation in the immediate vicinity of Victorville and possibly even more farther from town. The year before, there had already been 40 good wells produced west of Victorville, with that number doubling within another year. One company had a contract for 25

Presumably the proprietor of this flourishing Victor Valley orchard, c. 1910s
Mohahve Historical Society

Carrie Story, born a slave, was a longtime resident of Victorville, where she did laundry for many residents and told fortunes for numerous visiting movie celebrities.
Mohahve I

wells. The estimate for Apple Valley at the time would be 20 wells, also easily doubled by 1914. The area between Oro Grande and Helendale was not far behind, besides the dozen wells being developed in Victorville proper. This was certainly a natural phenomenon, stimulated by earlier success and reports of apparently unlimited ground-water supplies. There is no indication of any government agency warning for restraint. However, despite widespread contemporary belief to the contrary, groundwater in any given aquifer is limited, particularly during years of little recharging by precipitation. It would not be long before some ranchers would begin to notice that, with the massive summer pumping, the water table had begun to drop. It is doubtful if many property owners retained sufficient optimism concerning prospects in the area to deepen their wells when they eventually went dry, but that would be a realistic prospect at some later juncture.

"Traction plow" used by Civil War veteran George Z. Smith to cultivate part of his 600-acre ranch, c. 1913
The Kingdom of the Sun

In the fall of 1913, Victor Valley landowners mounted new efforts to secure government assistance in developing a Mojave River irrigation system. John D. Reavis, representing the local reclamation committee, and Arthur Hull, president of the area chamber of commerce — both partners in the largest real estate promotion and sales firm operating in the valley — traveled to San Francisco to confer with new President Woodrow Wilson's Secretary of Interior, Californian Franklin K. Lane. They outlined an optimistic plan to irrigate 175,000 acres of land with water reclaimed from the northern watershed of the San Bernardino Mountains, asserting it was one of the "most meritorious irrigation projects to be found in the West." Received warmly by the cabinet member, they were informed the reason the state had not been given her "full quota" of reclamation allocations was that there had not been sufficient worthy applications. While explaining that all current funds were committed elsewhere, the procedures for effective submission were recommended, with encouragement that a bill was pending in Congress for more reclamation appropriations.

The delegation also met California Sen. John B. Works, whom they found sympathetic and well informed about their venture and willing to support efforts in its behalf. Among the major complications of the project discussed with the senator was that most of the water in question was claimed by several large corporations, particularly the Appleton Land, Water and Power Company and the Arrowhead Water and Power Company, which recently had efforts to divert water through the mountains to San Bernardino blocked by the higher California courts. That company was certainly not ready to give up on the millions of dollars invested without proper reimbursement — hopefully by the federal government. It became evident the Arrowhead company was perfectly willing to divest of its interests to a private company as well, if such a buyer could be located. Subsequent efforts also proved unsuccessful and eventually U.S. entrance into World War I stalled prospects for such projects indefinitely.

Some of the 500 guests who reportedly gathered at the Hull ranch, c. 1913
The Kingdom of the Sun

Hesperia Hotel in 1916
Hesperia: A Pictorial History

Throughout the period, attempts to obtain an irrigation system were spearheaded by real estate promoters who stood to profit most from its accomplishment. But individual landholders and entrymen were equally optimistic of personal profits. There were but few involved who were not at least partially motivated by the speculative mood in vogue in the era. Hull and Reavis' California Land and Water Company advertised Victor Valley land at $15 to $25 per acre and offered the "most reliable list of desirable pear, apple and alfalfa properties." Another Los Angeles-based firm of McDonald and Gill advertised that the valley could offer home seekers much more for their money than could be obtained anywhere else in Southern California.

Arthur Hull, a Southern California real estate man claiming 40 years of experience, backed the local booster newspaper, the Victor Valley *News Herald,* from near its inception and certainly understood the role it could play in generating land sales. He also exerted elaborate efforts to make his own large Apple Valley ranch a model "horticultural station." He not only displayed all of the evidences of prosperity through successful farming techniques, but also experimented in determining what could most successfully be produced in the area. In 1913 he added a thousand cherry trees to his extensive already-maturing orchards. The cherry trees partly served as a windbreak in the center of the property, which was also enclosed by four miles of fence and an outer windbreak of 4,000 Mt. Rayle Cypress trees. That fall he planted 320 acres of newly cleared land to winter wheat. Exotic plants, such as Sudan grass from Africa, were also grown. The ranch wells had always impressed the numerous visitors who had occasion to observe the flows. There was a 25,000-gallon raised tank to provide water pressure for indoor plumbing to most of the 17 buildings on the ranch, including the 11-room main house, which featured a solar water heater. Many of his 35 employees were engaged in making and laying concrete pipe, aiming to convey water from the large storage reservoir to all parts of the ranch. Eventually he succeeded in divesting himself of the ranch, for a reported quarter-million dollars, just as the land boom began to wane.

Inside the Hesperia Hotel, with perhaps the same piano on which Paderewski performed an informal concert when stranded there by a snowstorm
Mojave River Valley Museum, Barstow, Helen Graves Collection

Aerial photo of Phelan,
c. 1940s
Mohahve V

Laying concrete pipes
for Adelanto orchard
irrigation, c. 1920
Adelanto: The Desert Transformed,
*donated by early community
pioneer Eddie Deutschmann*

Another method of encouraging local fruit growers and boosting the area to outsiders was to enter apples produced in Victor Valley in statewide fairs and shows. In 1913 the chamber of commerce dispatched an experienced showman, D.W. McPhereson, with a collection of good local products to Watsonville where he set up an exhibit amidst those of far better-known apple-growing regions of California. The high desert apples won two blue and two red ribbons, considered more than admirable for a newly established growing area.

Other sections of Victor Valley were being developed as well, although with fewer land claimants. By 1913 Mirage Valley, mainly west of future Adelanto, had a clubhouse that soon functioned as a school. An improvement association of 40 members studied alfalfa production and well-pumping machinery. To the southwest a community named Baldy Mesa, limited by scarce water, sought to produce fruit, eventually with some success. By 1915 settlers farther southwest, near the edge of the valley, had organized the Sheep Creek Water Company and sought to bring water from the future Wrightwood area to what would soon be named Phelan. Floods and engineering challenges discouraged plans for irrigation, but a flourishing community emerged nevertheless.

There had been some homesteaders in what became Adelanto — first called Sunrise Valley — since the first years of the century. By 1911 there was sufficient population for 25 charter members to organize a women's organization, which for a half-century thereafter was known as the Fremont Club. Initially something of a literary group, members submitted items for consideration of publication in *The Kingdom of the Sun,* a surprisingly good booklet-magazine aiming to "boost" the desert region. The community organized a school district in 1913 and soon erected a school located just a few large blocks west of the present Adelanto city hall.

Around 1914 Earl H. Richardson, inventor of the Hotpoint electric iron, manufactured by a company in Ontario, California, began developing the lands between Sunrise Valley and the Mojave River. He established what was called the Home Ranch on the main road from Victorville to Mirage Valley, soon named Crippen after his first property manager. At least seven wells were drilled from which water was pumped 150 feet to the surface to be stored in two concrete reservoirs with a capacity of a half-million gallons. A distribution system of locally manufactured concrete pipe was laid to convey water, primarily to irrigate deciduous fruit trees. Many of these trees were soon planted on the Richardson property. In keeping with the community founder's persistent preference for Hispanic flavor, the projected town was named Adelanto, meaning to advance or go ahead. It was said by the promoters to indicate the prevailing spirit of the endeavor. A post office was started under that name early in 1917, with J.C. Howard, also the town storekeeper, in charge. Thus was founded the last of the Victor Valley towns.

Fruit trees and electric power lines, which implied an abundance of water and modernity, lined the streets of the Adelanto townsite, c. 1920.
Adelanto: The Desert Transformed, *donated by Eddie Deutschmann*

While the promoters would never have admitted it publicly, the water supply from area wells was inadequate for the growth they anticipated. They wisely solved the problem through the Adelanto Fruit Company purchasing part of the pioneer Turner Ranch situated below the mesa near the Mojave River. This included one of the best water rights in Victor Valley, including a series of natural seeps called Adelanto Springs and probably some claims

Earl Richardson's "Home Ranch" showing a variety of deciduous fruit trees with an alfafa field in the background, c. 1920
Adelanto: The Desert Transformed, *donated by Eddie Deutschmann*

Southwestern Portland Cement Company plant shortly after it was established in 1914 *"Shades of Victor Valley," Victorville Branch, San Bernardino County Library, Collection of Jeff Goodwill (late mayor of Victorville)*

to the river flow. By the summer of 1924, a centrifugal pump and a 75-horsepower engine capable of lifting water 200 feet through a concrete pipe into the existing Adelanto irrigation storage and distribution system, were installed in a pump house erected on the new property. This was a significant development, assuring the future of the community despite all subsequent difficulties. With this improvement, agricultural production was a more realistic possibility. The installation was financed, as were most aspects of the town-building operation, largely by Richardson. It was stipulated that each land purchaser would also need to own the proportion of water stock needed to irrigate his orchard.

By 1924 pear production brought excellent market prices. The Adelanto growers erected a good packing, cold storage and processing facility. During the 1925 season they produced 20,000 gallons of apple cider and grape juice — perhaps more in demand during prohibition among people seeking to ferment their own alcoholic beverages. That year the company packed 400 tons of fresh fruit.

After adequate experimentation with building materials, Richardson's crews began constructing small adobe houses on 2.5-acre lots to sell to prospective orchardists. He then engaged successful promoters to sell the Adelanto agricultural subdivision lots among Los Angeles buyers. A new three-room schoolhouse of Spanish-style architecture was also built in 1925.

In the late summer of 1914, Carl Leonardt, reputedly the world's largest cement producer controlling the large Southwestern Portland Cement plant at El Paso, Texas, announced intent to begin construction of a similar facility at Victorville. He had already acquired the essential limestone quarries situated northeast of town and aimed to build a local plant with a capacity of 2 million sacks of cement annually. The company established a cordial relationship with officials of the Appleton Land, Water and Power Company, securing what land was necessary about a mile west of the center of Victorville. The company soon started work on an essential spur railroad, named the Mohave Northern, to the quarry from the plant situated adjacent the Santa Fe-San Pedro, Los Angeles and Salt Lake City main line.

The Appleton company certainly profited from the erection of the cement plant, expected to employ 200 workers and bring a thousand new residents to town, more than doubling its population. Owning 30,000 acres of mostly vacant land in the vicinity, it stood to gain substantially from this growth. The first week that such lands were for sale, the company sold more than $8,000 worth of property. Two years later it

Guests and townspeople at the dedication of Mojave Northern Railroad, built by Southwestern Portland Cement Company to haul limestone from its quarries some five miles away *"Shades of Victor Valley," Victorville Branch, San Bernardino County Library, Collection of Jeff Goodwill*

was determined that 71 of 124 residences within the town limits, which probably extended no farther than Tracy Street, had been constructed within the past three years, half in the past three months. This did not include a considerable number of residences that consisted of tents and tent houses, some with board sides. Soon afterward, the company developed a municipal waterworks tapping the natural seeps at the foot of the bluff immediately west of the town center. By simply digging a ditch and collecting the flow from some six artificially improved springs, they pumped a then adequate water supply into a storage tank on top of the bluff. The company also installed a town water delivery system.

In 1916 one-third of the 28 business houses in Victorville were new in the past three years. The Richardson brothers, Ervin E. and Walter W., "Big and Little Rich," had come to Victor in 1897, establishing their store and transportation business, which had prospered markedly. The Turner store, established in 1899, carried such a large variety of goods that its ads compared the establishment to a large city department store. A Victor Valley Mercantile opened that year with free refreshments and grafanola music in the new Vandever building on the corner of Seventh and D streets, which also housed a garage, grocery store and the post office. In 1917 a large new Stewart Hotel was added to the two others still operating, and there were several flourishing cafes. With cooperation from cement plant officials, former Anaheim banker Elton Goble opened the First National Bank of Victorville, much appreciated by the townspeople.

In 1916 the community received electric service from Southern Sierra Power Company, later organized into Southern California Edison. That year T.H. McDonald's wife operated a 10-room Victor Valley Hospital on 7th Street, including a well-lit operating room. Rev. Oliver M. Butterfield organized a Methodist Episcopal church and supervised construction of a house of worship. Years later he confessed this had been located as far from the boisterous antics of the cowboy saloon as he could get it, saying the town was truly wild while admitting many good people resided there. In early 1916 Father Brady of San Bernardino commenced regular Roman Catholic services at Victorville, though it would be another dozen years before the parish church would be completed.

Stewart Hotel on Seventh Street in Victorville, 1910-1920
Mohahve Historical Society

Southern Sierra Power Company's 60-foot steel towers brought electric power to Victor Valley, c. 1916.
The Kingdom of the Sun

In the fall of 1913 the Santa Fe Railroad donated land adjacent the track right-of-way from Fourth Street to the lumberyard at Seventh Street. The expressed purpose was for the townspeople to establish a horticultural park to demonstrate the plants that could be effectively grown in the high desert. The railroad also provided the irrigation water essential to accomplish that goal. Forrest Ackley, who with his father operated the neighboring lumberyard, volunteered to plan much of the park and devoted considerable time to its care. When the young man died some time later, the park was named for him. There were periodic community and railroad employee projects to improve the park, much appreciated by tourists as well as townspeople. Many community celebrations were held there.

With citizens specifically rejecting town incorporation, the local chamber of commerce semisuccessfully lobbied for better county roads, reorganized a more efficient volunteer fire department and organized the movement for a Victor Valley high school. After an effective bond campaign, the main buildings were erected, considered modern in every way when completed in 1917. The high school would long afterward serve as the Victor Junior High. Within a decade a hundred students attended the secondary school facility.

By that time the elementary school population had doubled. Classes were taught in rented rooms and temporary buildings, much criticized by newspaper editor Clifford Moon for the false economy. He correctly argued this situation would not be tolerated in many places. A new school was finally approved in 1922, still standing as Old Victor School. Soon after, a smaller Eva Dell school was added across the railroad tracks expressly for the minority children residing there.

The new high school for Victor Valley in 1917, which later became Victor Junior High
Mohahve Historical Society

Cliff Moon, publisher/editor of the Victor Valley *News Herald* in the early 1940s, was also instrumental in securing San Bernardino County Fair for Victorville.

Victor Valley College Library Local History Collection, donated by Jean Goldbrandsen

5 CHAPTER FIVE 1917-1955

Recurrences of War, Disappointments, Recovery and Development

(Opening photo)
Marie Chapule, longtime Paiute Indian resident of Victorville, lived more than a century.
"Shades of Victor Valley," Victorville Branch, San Bernardino County Library, Jeff Goodwill Collection (late mayor of Victorville)

Soon after the United States entered World War I, the county called on its eligible men to register for the draft. In late August 1917 the first 25 area men, more than two-thirds of whom were from Victorville, were called up by the lottery process. Prior to induction, the men were honored at a community send-off dance at the high school. In the ensuing year, a considerable number of local men were sent to the western front of France and Belgium. Army Capt. Allen Fletcher was soon a decorated hero of the Argonne Forest campaign. By the end of September 1918, 117 valley men had gone into the service, with at least 80 more joining prior to the ensuing armistice on November 11. While others returned home, Fred McDougall succumbed to pneumonia in Virginia while awaiting release from the service. The first Victor Valley American Legion Post was thereafter named in his honor. Army Sgt. J.S. "Sol" Ursenhall, a former employee on the Rogers ranch and one of the first to leave Victorville for the war, died in France of complications from battle wounds just two weeks after the conflict ended.

As the nation entered the war, citizens of Victor Valley formed patriotic societies to encourage assistance on the home front. The most significant was the local chapter of the American Red Cross. The Appleton Land, Water and Power Company offered free irrigation water to Victorville residents willing to plant "victory gardens" to help reduce demands for food that might otherwise be shipped to American boys and their allies in Europe. Victorville banker Elton Goble, deferred from military service, led in promoting the sale of war bonds. In the first bond drive, Victorville received an honor flag for being the first town in San Bernardino County to surpass its quota of "Liberty Loan" subscriptions.

War casualties weren't the only cause of sorrow. Although records are far from complete, it appears that Victor Valley was extremely fortunate to avoid most of the devastation of the worst modern epidemic in the history of Spanish influenza. It cost far more lives in the United States than did the war casualties. The first death known to have occurred was young Lula May Fleener of Baldy Mesa. Records of the matter are scarce, but there were at least four other casualties known in Hesperia.

The efforts to get federal government assistance with the Mohave River irrigation project, which had begun in 1913, had been put on hold by the World War I government-preparedness crusade. But a fateful division of most area landowners into two project groups based on location of their farms proceeded nevertheless. One project was primarily for people occupying the east mesa around Apple Valley. It featured a proposed storage reservoir at the forks where the Mojave River converged near the mouth of Deep Creek. The other project, which would irrigate the west mesa of Hesperia, Baldy Mesa and lands south and west of Victorville, aimed to utilize the Little Bear Valley Reservoir, already called Lake Arrowhead, for its primary water storage. This latter group organized as Victor Valley Mutual Water and Power District to quietly pursue its ends. The president of the company, F.M. Walton of Los Angeles, cautioned against a "sectional feeling" toward its Apple Valley neighbors. He warned that ill-timed criticisms made without full knowledge of the facts would demonstrate discord in the valley, which might handicap efforts to benefit all entrymen and landowners. Failure to heed this advice proved the most definite reason government funds were never allocated for a Mojave River irrigation project. Soon landowners on each side of the river organized to press their rival plans. Both irrigation districts presented petitions to the county board of supervisors insisting on action even though that body had informed them there wasn't sufficient information for a proper judgement on the crucial matter. Victor Valley landowners essentially forced the Mojave River Commission, which was formed for the purpose of investigating the feasibility of the proposed irrigation projects without the prospect of federal government assistance. Area landowners and entrymen were apparently so desperate to resolve that they were willing to risk a negative report based on less than complete data. Undoubtedly, many recognized they had filed on more federal land than they could prove up on without such water. This had to be a major factor in what otherwise appears to have been unwise actions. Prodding a group of engineers into a month-long study was not the way to elicit a report favorable to the fund-raising and promotion efforts essential for government assistance. Those experts understood the matter should have much more data collection and analysis.

The commission report was predictably negative. It focused on the water claims of the various entities, including the still-extant large corporations, and the inflated estimates of how much water was actually available in the river basin. The major conclusion of the river commission was that the various factions within Victor Valley must come together and agree upon an acceptable plan to allocate and distribute the surplus waters of the Mojave River. Otherwise it would be many years — if ever — before significant expanded agricultural development of the area would occur. This simply was not accomplished. The most significant outcome of the uncertain Victor Valley water situation was that federal land officials had been directed to reject all annual and final proofs on desert land entries that were based on ownership in the local water companies or on anticipated water delivery from those companies. Thus the failure to agree on water allocation doomed most of the Victor Valley homesteads established over more than a decade. Prospects for a flourishing agricultural district, which had commenced with such optimism, now virtually collapsed. It may also be argued, however, that the real cause of failure

In 1928 the Lone Wolf Colony was significant in part for bringing electricity and phone service to south Apple Valley.
"Shades of Victor Valley," Victorville Branch, San Bernardino County Library, Eve Farry Collection

Mrs. Ray Moore feeding chickens at the Adelanto homestead she and her husband established in the 1920s
Mohahve Historical Society

was the lack of flow consistency on the Mojave River, which has continued to discourage large-scale irrigation development in the region to the present time.

There would still be successful agricultural enterprises in the area, particularly along the Mojave River, but valley citizens were essentially forced to diversify their economic endeavors, which they did with success. In the 1920s Adelanto became a major poultry producing center. Again E.H. Richardson played a crucial role, encouraging experimentation and education in methods of producing turkeys, chickens and eggs. The livestock industry actually expanded over what it had been in earlier years. Later in the decade dairying appeared about to became a major enterprise in the area.

Movie star William S. Hart rescuing a damsel in the Upper Mojave Narrows around 1920
"Shades of Victor Valley," Victorville Branch, San Bernardino County Library, Jeff Goodwill Collection

Another important Victor Valley industry was movie making. In the two decades before and after World War I, a large number of pictures were filmed on location in the Victor Valley. William S. Hart, who considered himself the first to depict the authentic cowboy life, chose to make most of his popular pictures there. Each film company visit transfused a considerable amount of money into the cash registers of hotels and restaurants, lumber companies and other businesses, in some cases up to $125,000 for one movie.

The Golden State Portland Cement Company plant in Oro Grande acquired an excellent reputation for its product, rated by the United States government as "cement of quality." Because of huge advance orders the plant was expanded. In 1923 it was purchased by the larger Riverside Cement Company. The Southwest Portland Cement plant at Victorville continued to be the industry showplace, as it, too, expanded capacity. By mid-1925, the two plants were producing 10,000 barrels of cement every day, a full third of the entire output of the industry in Southern California and certainly the largest enterprise of the Victor Valley.

Both cement plants employed Mexican-American and African-American laborers whose families resided in nearby communities, often in neighborhoods separated from the majority of white residents. One of these was in the oldest part of Victorville, near E Street, northeast of the railroad tracks. An African-American community also began in the Bell Mountain area north of Apple Valley. There were always a few Native Americans living in close proximity to other area citizens as well. The minority population interacted reasonably well with their neighbors, but not yet on terms of full equality.

There is little evidence that small homesteads prospered from the planting of fruit trees prior to the 20s. However, some of the better-financed larger landowners

Apples grown by Mr. Phillips on the Rhodes Ranch about 1924
Mohahve I

did well during the period. Most of the successful ranches were in Apple Valley, although there were also several below Oro Grande. In 1925 at least a half-dozen ranches made real profits. Their pears, peaches and apples not only commanded premium prices from discerning buyers but also won an impressive array of ribbons at the Los Angeles County Fair in Pomona that and the following year.

Victorville continued to develop as a regional center. Besides railroad shipping and expanded tourist facilities, commercial establishments included at least four department or general stores and an equal number of grocery and butcher markets. In 1926 private investors added a 20-bed hospital in a new Spanish-style structure just west of the cement plant on the highway just becoming Route 66. The number of church congregations and meeting places also proliferated during the decade. As in other places, the high school remained the focus of much community interest.

But whatever prosperity the region enjoyed during the 20s, it was brought to a rather abrupt halt as the new decade approached. The deciduous fruit industry that had recently made Victor Valley quite famous died almost completely. While there have been other explanations, it was mainly a combination of lack of viable markets as the Depression dropped prices along with the ravages of disease. Tree diseases and insects, eliminated the flourishing orchards so completely that many later residents refused to believe fruit production could ever have been impressive.

Even more devastating was the failure of the local bank the week before Christmas in 1931. The Marsh family, which had recently operated the institution, may have invested too much of the funds in questionable enterprises, including movie making. Some believed the family's interest in out-of-town activities such as sailing left the business poorly managed. Although most depositors eventually received back two-thirds of their funds, there was much shock, bitterness and inconvenience experienced as was the case in most communities across the country.

The Depression dislocated many people. Although editor C.M. Moon never mentioned overloaded old automobiles of migrant families like the Joads in the fictional *Grapes of Wrath*, townspeople were not as cordial to such travelers as had been the case earlier. The local law enforcement personnel were assigned to drive them out. On the other hand, Victor Valley citizens demonstrated not only compassion but also impressive community

(Far left)
Verde-Kemper Campbell Ranch main house designed by John Byers and built between 1927 and 1929
Victor Valley College Library Local History Collection

Civilian Conservation Corps camp, 1933 to 1940, at Miller Canyon site of later Lake Silverwood
Victor Valley College Library Local History Collection

Green Spot Deluxe Motel, an amazingly modern tourist facility, built by John Roy in 1937
"Shades of Victor Valley," Victorville Branch, San Bernardino County Library, Jeff Goodwill Collection

spirit in assisting fellow residents in need during this difficult time. Canvases for food and clothing helped, as did distribution of surplus flour and cloth. One of the most impressive citizens, Imogene Garner Hook, sponsored Christmas parties for all school-aged children and for at least three years made certain each had at least one present.

The increasing hardships created by the Depression spurred national social reform. With the coming of Franklin D. Roosevelt's New Deal, local road building through the Civil Works Administration provided up to a hundred jobs to family heads. While the Civilian Conservation Corps aimed primarily at employing young men from the southern and eastern cities, the personnel assigned to camps in the nearby San Bernardino Mountains markedly improved roads, livestock grazing and recreational facilities used by Victor Valley residents.

Beginning in late 1933 community activists commenced efforts to construct a high school gymnasium with assistance from federal work programs. It took some five years but the result was built to last for the ages. It is the foremost monument to the New Deal and local support in the high desert. Assistance from the Works Progress Administration also helped improve Victorville's potable water system and thus its fire protection to a high level of efficiency.

Midway through the 30s, Victor Valley began some semblance of recovery from the Depression. The cement orders from Boulder-Hoover Dam construction and the huge electric power line construction project associated with it injected a good deal of funds and employment in the area. However, the main factor bringing about a return to prosperity was the vast development of the tourist industry in Victor Valley. Americans in great numbers took their automobiles over the relatively new Route 66 (later Interstate Highway 40) and Arrowhead Trails Highway (later Interstate Highway 15), which converged not far from Victorville. Before long there were a dozen eating establishments and 17 service stations spread along the popular highway. New motels were added including the Green Spot Deluxe Motel built in 1937 with modern air conditioning.

There had always been interest in recreation, organized and otherwise in the valley. The Depression-era government programs enhanced this, including the construction of tennis courts and a replacement swimming pool at the high school. A country club, including a golf course, continued to be developed near the historic Turner Ranch at Adelanto Springs. Softball was also avidly supported by numerous teams playing throughout the summers. But the event for which Victor Valley became most famous was the annual nonprofessional rodeo started in 1934. After state-relief-administration crews helped remove a stand of cottonwood trees from Santa Fe Railroad property near Forrest Park, seats were installed and an arena constructed to serve both ball players and cowboys and their spectators. By the second year of the rodeo, word had spread and a large array of movie stars and other celebrities attended in 1936, some participating as officials and otherwise. By 1937 the event attracted at least 10,000 people. But soon after, the best of the cowboy participants joined the new professional "Turtle Association" and began seeking major prize money at Eastern rodeos during the fall season when the local event had been held. In addition, some members of the chamber of commerce who had helped sponsor the rodeo became apprehensive about

One of numerous area horse races, December 1914

Victor Valley College Library Local History Collection, Arlene Kallenberger Collection

liability problems, leading them to withdraw support. There was no rodeo in 1939, although the leading promoter, Cal Godshall, hosted one the following spring at his Apple Valley ranch featuring college students. This has sometimes been considered the first-ever intercollegiate rodeo. Most rodeos faded from the area as wartime approached, although they returned during the ensuing decades.

Another notable development involving celebrities was the proliferation of "dude" guest ranches. The old Verde Ranch, owned by the Kemper Campbell family since 1924, began hosting paying customers, profiting from what had been an informal arrangement for years. The industry actually started with Catherine Boynton and Dr. Katherine Evans at their homestead, the Yucca Loma Ranch in Apple Valley, long-operated by Boynton's daughter, Gwen Behr. Many movie stars, including Clark Gable, stayed at both places. Another significant property was that of Murray's Dude Ranch. It catered to African-American customers, including reigning heavyweight boxing champion Joe Louis, who was pictured there in the new *Life* magazine in late 1937. The industry was even more extensive in the decade after World War II.

The worst flood on the Mojave River since Victor Valley was settled occurred in March 1938. It was particularly devastating to the Mexican-American community east of the railroad tracks, with an estimated 25 to 30 homes destroyed. Warning was sufficient for evacuation to churches and other buildings in safer areas, so there was little loss of life. Farmlands along the river were also

Yucca Loma Guest Ranch cottage built by Ernest Thompson Seton, author of nature books for boys and early official of the Boy Scouts of America
Victor Valley College Library Local History Collection

washed away in many areas and the railroad grade through the Upper Mojave Narrows was obliterated. The county allocated funds to rebuild bridges and the Army Corps of Engineers commenced long term plans to alleviate such a hazard in the future.

Early in 1940, many began anticipating the United States entrance into World War II, including Victor Valley *News Herald* editor Clifford Moon. Some local young men, including at least a half-dozen Mexican-Americans, enlisted in the service. The Hispanic servicemen received a dinner-dance send-off traditional in the area during the previous war. At least two of these men lost their lives in the subsequent military engagements. However, community residents were proud to have participated in this important crusade for freedom.

Just prior to Pearl Harbor, some civic leaders accompanied officials of the Civil Aeronautic Authority that were inspecting various localities in the area for a possible flying school field. Many understood that desert weather conditions were generally ideal for pilot training. Some hoped that since federal work projects were still being funded they could secure such assistance for the field. In September 1940 the county board of supervisors authorized a committee to obtain options on a section of land just east of Adelanto for a U.S. Army-approved flying school. For a time a Los Angeles syndicate planned to develop what was called Victor Air Institute. That fall, American Legion and other volunteers refurbished a formerly-used municipal air strip just south of Victorville, anticipating private flying lessons to be offered there.

When the flying school concluded not to exercise its option to build the institute, local chamber of commerce leaders Guy Johnson and Dr. J.O. Moore in April 1941 went directly to Army Air Corps officials to attempt to generate interest in a Victor Valley base. Within two months the War Department authorized over $5 million to establish one of the largest training bases then being planned in the nation at the expanded Adelanto site. Groundbreaking took place in July with runway paving, hangar construction and other projects under way. All involved anticipated the arrival of 250 twin-engine

Guests arriving at Murray's Dude Ranch in Apple Valley
Ebony, February 1947

Jim Sprinkle and girlfriends at lush Deep Creek location during the summer before the flood of 1938 scoured out much of the topsoil for such vegetation
"Shades of Victor Valley," Victorville Branch, San Bernardino County Library, Allison Stockdale Collection

Historic railroad grade through Upper Mojave Narrows after the river changed course during the great flood of 1938
"Shades of Victor Valley," Victorville Branch, San Bernardino County Library, Jeff Goodwill Collection

Eva Dell School, fifth and sixth grades, 1945
"Shades of Victor Valley," Victorville Branch, San Bernardino County Library, Felix Diaz Collection

Loading practice bombs at Victorville Army Air Base early in World War II.
Victorville Army Air Base Annual, 1942
Victor Valley College Library Local History Collection

training planes. The first service personnel came from Mather Air Station near Sacramento under the command of Maj. William B. Offutt. A group of bomber-pilot trainees began their last phase of instruction just after the

Chow line at relatively new Victorville Army Air Base
Victorville Army Air Base Annual, 1942
Victor Valley College Library Local History Collection

Japanese attack on Pearl Harbor and graduated in April 1942. The base functioned throughout the war as a bombardier school, also training many other top-flight fighting personnel, including bomber, glider and fighter pilots and later in the war, radar operators.

As the Victorville Army Air Field became operational, community leaders, including Imogene Hook, began efforts to build a U.S.O. facility in Victorville. Appleton Land and Water Company donated a lot on Eighth Street and construction soon began.

Dances and other social activities were consistently staged there. The night that local citizens learned their nation was at war, they instituted a blackout for the early evening. Such blackouts were thereafter strictly enforced by the Victor Valley justice of the peace. Others consistently manned listening posts to warn of approaching unidentified aircraft. And the community again cooperated markedly in war bond sales, salvage drives and accepting the necessary rationing of scarce commodities. Area housing remained in particularly short supply but there was cooperation in room rental and construction of quarters for service personnel.

Far more men served in this than in the earlier world war, with some seeing action in the South Pacific, the Philippines, Okinawa, Anzio Beach in Italy and within Germany itself. Several were cited for valor and some half dozen gave their lives in the supreme sacrifice for their country. Victor Valley had two newspapers by this time. Neither did particularly well reporting on most of the local servicemen's wartime assignments.

Even after the war ended, some in the area continued to struggle with materials shortages. Local baker Tony Zanetti blamed the federal price regulating and rationing agency, Office of Price Administration (OPA), for his inability to secure sufficient sugar. Relatively new Victor *Press* Editor John Barry had recently denounced the OPA as unnecessary, although others asserted it prevented massive price gouging as demand and ability to pay any price greatly outstripped supply.

Barry proved more accurate when he stated "we don't know where the real estate promoters fit into the scheme [of the future of the area], but we definitely recognize

Baker and local rodeo promoter Tony Zanetti with friends in front of his business establishment in the late 1940s
Mohahve Historical Society

their potency to change the whole direction and scope of our steady growth." The editor could not possibly have known how accurate his prediction was. Despite the definite negative aspect of the ensuing real estate boom, the work of land promoters in Victorville, Apple Valley and Hesperia, most notably that of Clyde Tatum, Newt Bass and Penn Phillips, would be the most important aspect of the valley's history in the 50s and for some time after that. The initial significant step in this process was the breaking up of land holdings of the old Appleton Land and Water Company in 1946.

Within a year after the war, several investor-builders sought to help alleviate Victorville's continuing housing shortage with apartment-type single-story structures situated on Highway 66 south of town, near where government sponsored trailer houses for service personnel had been located several years before. By the next year, a half-dozen Federal Housing Authority and G.I. Bill-financed homes were under construction, with more than a dozen other such loan applications being processed.

The school population continued to reflect the rapid growth in the area, with the total enrolled in Victorville by 1950 at 1,314, up from 778 the fall after the war ended. Voters willingly approved the school building bonds presented to them. But the facilities could not be constructed quickly enough to alleviate overcrowding. As soon as possible, a new elementary school, named for the current superintendent, Harvey Irwin, was built at what was then the southwest corner of the expanding community. Del Rey Elementary School was soon planned farther west in what was then the most active housing subdivision area. The high school district recognized the need for a junior high and they soon concluded that a new high school was the best solution. The younger students inherited the older facility as a junior high. A bond election for the new high school passed in September 1951, with construction completed in spring 1954. Persistent hearsay asserts that some citizens believed the new school was located too far from the business center of town. But the contemporary newspapers did not reflect that concern, and situating the high school where it is demonstrated impressive foresight as to where the center of the community would be for a long time thereafter.

In the postwar era, the county government continued to operate marginally for the Victor Valley, although there were several discussions about creating a new desert county. Alleged neglect occasionally spurred discussion of incorporating Victorville as a city. Failure of a county official to attend a public health-related meeting was blamed for delay in extending sewer service across the tracks to lower-income housing in a timely manner. County road officials were instrumental in appropriating $94,000 to accomplish the long-desired grading and straightening of the highway from the Mojave Narrows Bridge toward Apple Valley. The same people played some role in widening the highway near Forrest Park, where trees and an old wall were removed. Other city streets received needed county allocations in 1951. At about the same time, the road from Hesperia to Route 66, ignored for many years, was paved largely because of the anticipated heavy use by potato-laden big trucks in the coming harvest season.

Shown here is Felix Diaz playing football on the Victor Valley High team in 1951. The school team played at an old field adjacent to the present junior high school. *"Shades of Victor Valley," Victorville Branch, San Bernardino County Library, Felix Diaz Collection*

Just after the war, in the fall of 1945, the Tatum brothers, Clyde, Alvin and Harry, along with partner Bob Walker, previously successful in similar endeavors in Perris Valley and Visalia, leased Appleton Land and Water acreage and water and began laying pipe for irrigating 500 acres. This soon became the largest potato field in southern California. With the exception of one drought year, the spud harvest exceeded 300 sacks per acre. The enterprise was sufficiently important to the host community that in some years of the Hesperia Days celebrations, a potato queen was crowned. The potato-growing operation continued to flourish into the 50s and doubtlessly laid the financial foundation for the same company's even more significant contribution to the valley later as the foremost real estate developers of Victorville.

Clyde and Alvin Tatum with part of a Hesperia potato crop that helped them become the foremost housing developers of Victorville *"Shades of Victor Valley," Victorville Branch, San Bernardino County Library, Jeff Goodwill Collection*

(Far right) Downtown area of Seventh Street, Victorville, c. 1960 *Victor Valley College Library Local History Collection, donated by Jean Goldbrandsen*

Capt. Joseph McConnell Jr., "triple jet ace," who shot down a record 16 enemy aircraft in the Korean War, had an Apple Valley home donated to his family prior to his death in an advanced test aircraft at nearby Edwards Air Force Base. *From Apple Valley promotional literature, Victor Valley College Library Local History Collection*

A year before the Korean conflict began, the Victorville Army Air Corps Base began to emerge from a prolonged period of semidormancy as an aircraft storage facility. In May 1949 funds arrived to help repair wind-damaged roofs of base buildings, and soon after plans were announced for new housing quarters for airmen and their families. This was necessary for the new base assignment to train neighboring states' air national guard flyers. As the base geared for this activity, about 50 F-51 Mustang fighter planes arrived for use. Soon after the United States became involved in the Korean War, about 75 F-86 Sabre jets were assigned to the base, just then being named for Brig. Gen. Harold H. George, hero of Bataan in the previous war. That summer of 1950, Victor Valley's National Guard tank battalion was called to active duty in the so-called police action. A year later, Bob Keiser of Oro Grande was wounded by an enemy mine and Don Hand was captured by the enemy. When the latter was finally released and returned home in 1953, some in the community helped him purchase a new Plymouth automobile. Besides the several national war heroes attached to George Air Force Base, namely jet pilot aces Joe McConnell and "Pete" Fernandez, the community had its own outstanding hero, Ricardo Cardenas, already decorated in World War II. He received a field promotion to second lieutenant and rallied his platoon to a decisive bayonet attack that took the assigned hill. He received a Silver Star and Korea's second-highest award for heroism.

In the summer after the war, Victor Valley citizens staged a flower show with an unprecedented 100 entries. The next year Victorville hosted what was billed as the "San Bernardino County Fair" in tents at Forrest Park. This was said to be a revival of a similar event held in 1930 and 1931 and was partly dedicated to the memory of newspaper editor Clifford Moon, killed in an automobile accident in Cajon Pass two years before. Moon had helped organize the earlier affair and demonstrated the foresight to obtain incorporation papers from county and state entities. This was fortunate because the next year Chino challenged Victorville's ability to host a proper county fair, although the San Bernardino Chamber of Commerce backed the desert community. The county and state both assisted with obtaining a 40-acre permanent fairgrounds. Volunteer labor commenced building the facility with subsequent state allocations eventually providing many permanent structures. In 1950 Governor Earl Warren helped with dedicating the fairgrounds. He mingled with up to 20,000 ticket holders attending that year, an increase from 11,000 the year before. In 1951 30,000 attended the well-staged affair, which once again included the always-popular horsemanship-related contests, along with agricultural, homemaking and mining exhibits. Yearly crowds reached 50,000 by the end of the decade. In the mid-1960s a racehorse track was added and, predictably, proved popular.

By that time several larger real estate development companies began building homes in tracts near the new fairgrounds. The Tatum Mesa Estates, located east across Highway 66-Seventh Street had erected at least 27 two- and three-bedroom houses by the late summer of 1950. A year later Penn Phillips, one of the leading land developers in the California Southland, opened a unit of his Mountain View Acres a half mile west of the main highway near Palmdale Road. In less than a month the Phillips company claimed they had sold 850 acres of housing lots. Another developer, Mervyn Hope, president of what was soon Home Savings and Loan, aimed to build up to a hundred houses. The Tatums also promoted a shopping center east of Highway 66, first featuring a new McMahan's furniture store and Hartwick Market, among others. Another developer was recent war veteran Verne Jester, who began building on 60 acres south of town.

Together these developers virtually shifted the town population center considerably to the south, encouraging businesses to locate along a greater extent of Seventh Street than before.

Early in the nationwide process of bypassing interstate traffic bottlenecks in city centers, which would soon be part of a unified Interstate Highway system, in February 1955 the state highway department accepted bids for a major highway bypass for Victorville. This began a mile north of Palmdale Road and continued to a half-mile north of First Street, including a substantial bridge across the Mojave. This was to be a four-lane highway featuring "big city"-type cloverleaf on-and-off ramps. The project raised questions about the impact on local tourism and other businesses, probably resulting in an overall negative economic effect as far as the tourism industry was concerned. However, a positive aspect can be discerned in that traffic flow and parking improved for local shoppers.

On February 22, 1946, brothers-in-law Newton Bass and "Bud" Westlund began selling Apple Valley Ranchos, acre homesites adjacent to Highway 18 north of most of the old Apple Valley ranches. With promotional ads in national magazines and many celebrities showing avid appreciation for the carefully planned community, much

The local beginnings of the Apple Valley Building and Development Company in 1946
The Golden Land of Apple Valley, California,
Mohahve Historical Society

Children at a party at Apple Valley Inn, c. 1949
Mohahve Historical Society

interest was quickly generated. In just over a year there were 1,200 property owners, with a considerable number of houses already under construction. A staff of a dozen Western-dressed salesmen kept interested clients more than informed. The main company offices were located at the new Apple Valley Inn by 1950. That facility became rather famous throughout California and beyond partly through the appearances of well-known orchestra leader, Freddy Martin.

As early as 1948 new residents considered the old elementary school inadequate and inconveniently located. When Bass donated sufficient land closer to his development, the school board resolved to construct a larger school there, later named Yucca Loma. A few of the older residents objected even though the newest segment of the earlier building was moved to the new site and temporarily utilized. The school bus schedule carefully assured good service to the older section of the community.

Even before World War II ended, many citizens of Victor Valley expressed a fervent desire for a good community hospital. After the war several companies and representatives of early prepaid health plans vied for favor in the high desert. In late 1946 some began fund raising, asserting that if each family donated a $100, a 20-bed hospital could be constructed. Despite several important contributions, including the cement plant, this effort faded for several years. A small indignity at the time was the sale of the old defunct hospital building erected in the 20s, which was to be remodeled as a hotel.

Finally, late in 1953 civic leaders, including land developers Newt Bass and Clyde Tatum, explained the options, including funds available through federal programs. Both developers had offered lots near their subdivisions, with Bass' parcel just north of Highway 18 being accepted. For a time there was an effort to have the county create a government hospital district. But before that materialized, interest shifted in favor of cooperating with the Sisters of the Immaculate Heart of Mary. Through Mother General Regina, the order pledged that it would assume management and full permanent responsibility for the facility as soon as it was constructed. Hospital backers debated this approach, but Bass asserted that more donations would be forthcoming if the government was not directly involved and voiced firm trust in the reliability of the Roman Catholic sisters. There were subsequently generous gifts, and although fund raising suffered small delays, a low bid of $511,000, including government funds, was accepted. Construction commenced on the facility which, with considerable expansions and assistance from other institutions later built, still serves the community well.

Hesperia's population growth had been stagnant for a full half-century, although in the early postwar era the Tatum potato operation partly stimulated and the economy. This changed dramatically in early 1954 when Penn

M. Penn Phillips, Hesperia developer, and his friend, former boxing champion Jack Dempsey, in 1954
Hesperia: A Pictorial History

additional $7 million to properly prepare the 36-square-mile tract. Seasoned promoters expected a seven-year process to bring the project to full fruition using promotional ads aimed primarily at Los Angeles-area radio and television users, along with celebrity-presence attention similar to what Apple Valley had profited from. Longtime Phillips friend, former boxing champion Jack Dempsey, was particularly visible. Predictably, a new elementary school was soon needed and built.

Unfortunately, the aggressive sales tactics of some sales people led to complaints to the Public Utilities Commission and the California Bureau of Real Estate. The charges to the former, dealing with reportedly inadequate water service, were no longer Phillips' responsibility and would have to be resolved through a long struggle to gain public control of what had always been a private water company. Phillips and several of his sales staff were accused of pointing to commercial possibilities of certain lots despite zoning prohibitions. The company head argued he did not know of

Phillips, with an illustrious group of financial associates, purchased the largest private land parcel to change hands in Southern California in 35 years. This secured 20,000 acres from the Appleton Land, Water and Power Company and the associated Lacey estate, reportedly for $1.25 million.

such practices if they occurred. But he was temporarily barred from selling real estate as were most of the others accused. Two were eventually banned from such sales for life. Phillips successfully withdrew from financial involvement with Hesperia at that point, but the stigma has, to

Community center at Lime Street Park, Hesperia, built by volunteer labor in the mid-1950s
Hesperia: A Pictorial History

6 CHAPTER SIX 1955-2000

Modern Era and Greatest Development

(Opening photo) A computer at Riverside Cement Company at Oro Grande with R.D. Hawley in charge — interested Japanese visited the plant in the 1950s. *Mohahve I*

After several periods of serious discussion of incorporation, in 1958 a Victorville cityhood movement commenced with the backing of three-fourths of the chamber of commerce. Those in favor argued taxes would actually decline. But opponents, mainly led by merchants from the downtown business district, opposed primarily for taxation reasons and eventually most, including the railroad and cement plant, were excluded from the proposed city limits. This helped defeat the issue in May 1959. But just eight months later, the matter emerged again, primarily because many influential citizens were convinced Victorville taxpayers paid for more than the services they received from the county.

First mayor of Victorville, Willard Wade (seated), was also president of the California Interstate Telephone Company prior to its purchase by Contel. *Victor Valley College Library Local History Collection, donated by Jean Goldbrandsen*

Conceding that the hesitant would never accept their arguments, proponents of incorporation retained an expert outside consulting firm to study the situation and report. Gold-Thompson of South Pasadena had recently recommended both for and against cityhood in other communities, and after a fund-raising period for local advocates to secure the necessary fee, the company was retained. Upon completion of the survey, the consulting firm recommended incorporation to unify and integrate the various government services the citizens were already paying for. They reported that with the new city receiving funds currently going to the county, taxpayers might well pay less after incorporation.

After voting five to one in favor of cityhood, the chamber of commerce took the last steps toward putting themselves out of the local government business by circulating the petitions essential to initiate an election through county channels. The incorporation vote was subsequently set for September 1962. There ensued some heated arguments both pro and con on the incorporation question, mainly about future taxes. The opponents drew primarily on examples from neighboring Barstow's current expenses. Incorporation was approved by a narrow 35-vote margin, 706 to 671, with telephone company official Willard Wade receiving the most city council votes and thus becoming the first Victorville mayor. Leading cityhood advocate Joseph Campbell garnered the second-highest vote and remained active in city government longest of the original council.

San Bernardino County officials promised full cooperation in the nine-month transition period, assuring that the sheriff's substation, library and justice court would remain in operation. David C. Williams, the public administrator who had directed the cityhood survey for the Gold company, stayed on as interim city manager and was later confirmed permanently in the office. Williams voiced his confidence that the city would be prepared to operate efficiently at the proper time and his admiration at the experience and willingness of the city council to do what was necessary to get the new government into operation. Council person Gladys Butts asserted that most former opponents of incorporation were already conceding the move for cityhood to be appropriate within weeks after the election. The first city offices were on Eighth Street, rented from Ray DeBlasis, and council meetings were held at the high school. The council contracted with the county sheriff for police service at a seemingly excellent price for the time.

One of the first city officials hired was the building inspector, who was immediately inundated with work. A great deal of the pressure came from Tatum's new Green Tree development, which was started about the same time as cityhood was voted in. Councilman Campbell termed the project one of the most important things that had ever occurred in Victorville. Indeed it eventually accounted for a large proportion of the homes in the south and eastern segments of the city. The infant city's officials attempted to cooperate with those continuing to develop subdivisions, understanding the need for further growth and increased assessed valuations.

This aerial view of Victorville in late 1960s was a gift from the Mohahve Historical Society to the Mojave River Valley Museum, Barstow.

One of the greatest challenges for the infant ctiy proved to be the sewer system, efficiently run through a special county district for a quarter-century before

Beginnings of Victorville Shopping Center, mid-1960s
Photo by Jean Goldbrandsen
Victor Valley College Library
Local History Collection

incorporation, but increasingly challenged to serve the demands of numerous new homes. Those involved understood the district functions would eventually be taken over by the city. In the meantime the city council and others debated about whether septic tanks could remain optional after several subdivisions ran into serious problems with inadequate percolation in the local soil. Leading developer Clyde Tatum conceded that connection to the sewer system was usually best but could not be economically feasible in all instances, unless perhaps subsidized by federal funds. Some smaller builders asserted that if they were compelled to extend main trunk sewer lines to their subdivisions, it would literally ruin them financially. The council thus delayed decision on such matters as the city continued to expand.

Steadily growing Apple Valley took a giant step toward the future form of her main business district when in 1961 the plan for a four-lane Highway 18 through the so-called village area was amended to include frontage roads. These roads would cost an additional $150,000 and were to be paid for by the property owners through a special assessment district. This was certainly a good way to solve the traffic and parking situation, though the arrangement continues to be somewhat confusing to all but local residents. Installment of 70 mercury vapor lights along the highway came in the spring of 1964. While the Apple Valley Building and Development Company (minus Bud Westlund and his sister, the former Mrs. Newton Bass) merged with Reserve Oil and Gas and was no longer as aggressive in local land promotion, other companies continued to open subdivisions. And Apple Valley residents in and near the Marianas foothills commenced a struggle with the seemingly oppressive Pacific Water Company. They finally won by creating their own municipal water company in 1962 and purchasing the private water system.

After building a third elementary school in the mid-1960s, the Apple Valley community was elated with the prospect of having its own high school by the fall of 1967. At this time there was no discussion of separating from the Victor Valley High School District, but the community had already seceded from Victorville and organized its own park and recreation department in 1952, succeeding impressively in the endeavor. The Apple Valley Community Center, completed in 1951, received major additions in 1962; and a new swimming pool, a joint effort of school, civic groups and the county, was completed at the junior high in 1963. Swimming became a major youth activity in the area thereafter. Golf remained popular in Apple Valley as the local country club developed and nationally known professionals, Lloyd Mangrum and Billy Casper, established residences nearby. There were also numerous equestrian activities in the area. The county library branch, opened in 1949, received a new facility adjacent to the offices of Dr. L.G. Ahntholz on Highway 18, where 1,800 patrons enjoyed 5,000 books in 1961.

Aerial view of Apple Valley High School under construction in 1967
"Shades of Victor Valley,"
Victorville Branch,
San Bernardino County Library,
Gary Stater Collection

By that time considerable commercial expansion had begun, and within two years the first apartment complexes were being constructed. The population was only 9,430 by the summer of 1966, but the infrastructure was in place, including ownership of a vast number of building lots. These lots would be developed during a relatively uneventful but larger building boom in the ensuing decades. Although there have been controversies over changing minimum lot size and whether to allow Wal-Mart to be established in Apple Valley, progress has continued with relative calmness. Apple Valley became a city in 1988 with endorsement of over 80 percent of the voters.

In the fall of 1964, the preliminary results of a survey of 18,000 Hesperia landowners indicated that 40 percent intended to build on their lots within a few years. Over 75 percent of those responding indicated intent to become permanent residents of the community. But in the meantime, Hesperia continued to struggle in several ways. The local Grange, the oldest organization in the community, attempted to take the lead in improving existing roads, a daunting task because of the vastness of the area and the large number of rather unimproved roads. Citizens almost lost their excellent private airport to a proposal for a public park on the property, although this did not come to fruition.

One of the most persistent issues facing Hesperia continued to be dissatisfaction with the local private water company. It became clear that Eastern stockholders in the Hesperia Water Company had no intention of making system improvements despite continued complaints. At one public meeting at that time a self-proclaimed witness alleged he had earlier, presumably in the Penn Phillips era, observed installation of pipe reclaimed from the oil industries, which he described as already rusty. While some citizen apathy persisted and even a small amount of opposition arose from a few, at the end of 1966 a county service area was created for the community. The first steps toward Hesperia self-government were thus launched through improving and expanding the water system. Hesperia's schools continued to develop as well, with a junior high and Hesperia High School well established prior to separation from the Victorville School District.

Even the best of water systems could not have helped much in the town's greatest crisis when in June, 1979 a wind-whipped brush fire cut a devastating swath of destruction a mile wide and three miles long through the south end of the community. Although at one point the fire was apparently headed for the business district, fire trucks and their crews, bulldozers cutting fire breaks and air tankers averted the threat. The conflagration came within a block of the main municipal fire station. At least 23 buildings were destroyed, an amazingly small number for the area burned. A decade later, some, including the libertarian editors of the *Daily Press,* occasionally opposed the expansion of fire protection others deemed essential.

Hesperia citizens decisively rejected incorporation in 1982, and a similar effort in 1986 never reached a vote. But the momentum for cityhood was building, as was desire for independence from any seeming domination by Victorville, evidenced by separation from the Victor Valley High School District at that time. Incorporation finally came in 1988.

One of the hallmarks of the Cold War era was the insecurity engendered among Americans because of the possibility of a nuclear attack on the United States. Besides ineffectually drilling

For years Hesperia motorists waited for trains at the Main Street intersection with the main Santa Fe Railroad line.
Later the viaduct-overpass solved the problem.
I Remember Hesperia: 1954-1974
by Myra McGinis

Sidewinder mine being refurbished as a civil defense bomb shelter in the mid-1960s
Victor Valley College Library Local History Collection, donated by Jean Goldbrandsen

school children to hide under their desks, more than a few constructed family bomb shelters. Civil defense personnel, both government and volunteer, sought means of preparing in some small way for such a catastrophe.

Annual groundwater-level monitoring program equipment used by the Mojave Water Agency in 1999
Water Resources Division, MWA

Several Victor Valley schools and the fairgrounds were equipped to serve as emergency hospitals. The county board of supervisors approved efforts to convert the old Sidewinder gold mine into a bomb shelter capable of protecting up to 800 persons, including medical and educational experts needed to rebuild a devastated community. Later, volunteers who worked sufficient hours building the facility reportedly received the right to places in the shelter if the terrible attack actually occurred. After a number of years, the premises was vandalized and eventually closed.

After all previous attempts to develop a major irrigation system in the Mojave River basin, in 1952 the powerful federal Reclamation Bureau decreed no water project was feasible there because no organization existed that could be responsible for allocating such water. It took that kind of shock and the renewed prospects of receiving at least some additional culinary water through the massive California Water Project to bring about the organization of the Mojave Water Agency (MWA). In 1961 the elected governing board of the MWA engaged an engineering firm to determine present water resources and needs and make plans to procure and allocate the anticipated additional resources. As plans were formed to bring an aqueduct through the area, in 1964 the local agency contracted with a prominent Riverside law firm to begin the process of adjudicating existing water rights, essential to determine future needs. Late the next year MWA attorney James H. Krieger reported good progress and unprecedented cooperation from virtually all major Mojave water users. The crucial process would also serve to protect existing rights from continued attempts by Lake Arrowhead Development Company and others to take more of the precious resource. Partly through the work of the MWA, the region was assured continued growth possible only through adequate water supplies.

The dam on the West Fork of the Mojave creating the Lake Silverwood segment of the state water system in 1972 did little to alleviate the threat of flooding the river had posed throughout history. However, the Mojave Forks Dam project, which had commenced soon after

Grading work began in 1964 to build Victor Valley College near the first library.
Panorama, 1969-70
Victor Valley College Library Local History Collection

the flood of 1938 and remained alive in the massive federal budgetary bureaucracy, has been more successful. In 1965 the Army Corps of Engineers requested formal agreements of cooperation on the project with San Bernardino County officials. There were subsequent budgetary scares and further delays, but eventually the dam came to fruition. Occasional unwise water releases from Lake Arrowhead during heavy rain runoff periods have caused some flooding, but the devastation of earlier years has essentially been eliminated by the project.

Similarly, after extensive study of the ancient riverbed, the Oro Grande Wash, and consideration of check dams and diversion into the Mojave River channel above the Upper Narrows, federal and county flood control experts agreed on another solution to the persistent threat of flooding in downtown Victorville. In early 1966 they concluded to construct an open drain between Center and Verde streets, covered from there to a point north of D Street. While this necessitated realigning Hesperia Road, it has effectively provided flood protection, although roads along the wash are still periodically closed and damaged during persistent precipitation periods.

In the late 1950s high desert residents became increasingly resentful of attempts to annex them into the San Bernardino Valley Junior College District, intending to draw tax funds for that purpose. When citizens recognized they were in fact paying to educate first-year college students from the area enrolled elsewhere, they realized there was very little financial difference between what they were already paying and what a local community college would cost. Particularly after Barstow chose to create its own junior college, the movement for a Victor Valley College became essentially assured. At first college classes were offered at the Victor Valley High School, whose administration and board of trustees also supervised the infant college. After considering up to 30 other possible college sites, the present college location on 237 acres of former South Verde-Kalin Ranch property was chosen in June 1962. This was a brilliant decision because of the central location among the feeder communities. The first cluster of buildings on the new campus was ready for use in the fall of 1965. The college continues to serve as a cultural center of the community as well filling important educational needs.

Although most residents never paid much attention, Victorville had its share of racial segregation for more than four decades. The 1960 census indicated 615 persons, almost all Mexican-American and African-American, residing in 195 dwellings in the E Street area. This comprised 6 percent of the community's labor force. In August 1962 civic and George Air Force Base leaders sponsored a public meeting to discuss the serious lack of housing facilities for low-income families seeking to live in the area. A Los Angeles newspaper catering to blacks alleged racial bias in the Victorville vicinity to be the reason minority families could not locate housing. During the three-hour meeting, realtors and builders argued that low-income housing was difficult to accomplish without government assistance. Sgt. Edwin D. Smith spoke for many when he stated that non-white servicemen took the same risks for their country as those who enjoyed easier housing availability, and they deserved better treatment.

The California attorney general was by then encouraging communities to pass anti-discrimination

Victor Valley business and professional women discussing issues in the mid-1960s. *Victor Valley College Library Local History Collection, donated by Jean Goldbrandsen*

instead of voluntarism. This was typical of the nationwide debates of the civil rights movement as most in the country became more aware of the need for racial equality. After this crisis, steady progress would be discerned in the matter of fair housing in Victor Valley as well equal opportunity in employment and education.

Victor Valley senior citizens first met to organize in September 1957, early in the nationwide movement for increasing awareness of this rapidly growing segment of the population. As the county geared up to serve seniors, Lovella Carling, a long-time advocate, was appointed coordinator of Senior Citizens for the Victor Valley County Services Council. In 1964 she and another activist, Pearl Pettis, attended a national convention in Chicago on related matters. They returned with a vision to establish a new senior citizens center to replace the one they had already outgrown on Sixth Street. Within less than two years, a much larger facility at Mojave Drive and Victor Street was in use and became a focal point for senior service projects benefiting the entire community. In later years the group continued to offer education, community service, fun, fellowship and a bridge between seniors and the community at large, and moved into a still larger center at a converted church building on Hesperia Road.

ordinances, which the state legislature did the following year. Some local citizens, particularly from the real estate industry, appeared alarmed when in 1963 this Rumford Act was enforced and supported repeal through the Proposition 14 initiative. Black realtor Goler V. Banks resigned from the local board of realtors when it supported this repeal. In 1964 a group of high desert "patriots" hosted John Birch Society regional functionary John Rousselot, who pointedly criticized government compulsion in desegregation,

Duncan Road crossing of the East Branch of the California Aqueduct in the Phelan area prior to construction of the MWA White Road siphon *MWA Third Annual Engineer's Report on Water Supply, 1996-1997*

Meanwhile, the Hesperia Leisure League, organized in 1962, attracted almost 200 active members in the first year. It soon acquired land between Fifth and Sixth streets on Main Street for a thrift shop and lounge. In May 1966 it also purchased seven acres on Third Street between Olive and Sultana with funds raised partly by selling lifetime memberships. It, too, proved impressive in its expansion of programs and facilities to meet member needs.

Despite the continued expansion and excellent service of St. Mary Hospital of Apple Valley, a 1960 survey indicated Victor Valley needed an additional 68 hospital beds. Even more would be needed to support anticipated future area development. A group that supported a Lutheran hospital in the San Fernando Valley of Southern

Victor Valley Community Hospital room and nurse, c. 1965

Victor Valley College Library Local History Collection, donated by Jean Goldbrandsen

The 35th Field Maintenance Squadron performing intermediate level maintenance on F-4 and F-105 aircraft at George Air Force Base, 1974
George Air Force Base

California offered to assist the community to construct the needed facility. With several prominent local citizens on the governing board, fund-raising commenced and a lot was obtained from the Kemper Campbell Ranch on the hill east of Hesperia Road and south of Verde Street in eastern Victorville. By March 1962, sufficient pledges were in place and the state hospitals agency gave approval for the $1.25 million project to be built by Tatum Construction Company.

Unfortunately, the 54-bed hospital encountered financial and other difficulties within four months of its opening. Soon both local citizens and physicians withdrew their support amidst growing opposition to out-of-town control. After closure, civic groups and the city of Victorville attempted to work out arrangements for reopening. But the question of more local control could not be resolved so long as the majority faction from the Pacoima, California, area remained dominant. Finally a group of other businessmen and physicians purchased the still-new facility, naming it Victor Valley Hospital and adding the term "community" soon after. Continued expansions in 1983, 1985 and 1996 brought the bed total to 122. But even in recent years difficulties continue to hang over this important institution.

During the post-Korean War era, George Air Force Base continued to serve as an important jet fighter training facility. In the fall of 1962, Capt. Charles E. Tofferi earned the worldwide Air Force title of top gun for his mastery flying of the F-104 Starfighter. The base soon received a number of F-105D Thunderbirds as well, making it the only American installation with all its aircraft capable of flying twice the speed of sound. One of the primary assignments of the U.S. Air Force during the Cold War era was to offer advanced pilot training to fliers from other allied nations. The George facility participated fully in this. As the country became more involved in the conflict in southeast Asia soon known as the Vietnam War, the base placed more emphasis on F-4C Phantom aircraft of the 476th Tactical Fighter Wing. As early as 1965 they commenced duty in Vietnam and witnessed their buddies killed in action. F-100 Super Sabre fighter pilots also saw duty early in this conflict. George Air Force Base remained an essential component of the area economy as well as of the national defense network even after the Vietnam War. A flying unit from the George base, proudly nicknamed the "Wild Weasels," played an important role in the later Gulf War. But that was the last prominence of the base.

An inevitable outcome of the collapse of the communist world and virtual end of the Cold War in Europe was a downsizing of the massive U.S. military establishment. It is not possible to state that politics played no role in

Busy Victorville business district in the early 1960s
Victor Valley College Library Local History Collection, donated by Jean Goldbrandsen

deciding which bases remained open, but a formula was established for facility closure. San Bernardino County was particularly hard hit, and Victor Valley lost what had become the major component of its booming economy when George closure was slated for 1992. It could be logically argued that the continued training of fighter pilots made more sense centered in the good weather conditions of an established base in the high California desert, rather than Mountain Home, Idaho, which had fewer good flying days and needed new base construction. But the decision was essentially automatic and irreversible. Thus ended a virtual love affair between a community and the Air Force at all levels.

A century after settlement of Victor Valley and many land promotion schemes later, valley growth took off, transforming the area into the beginnings of a major metropolis. After many decades of sporadic development led by Victorville in the 1970s and even more in the 1980s, Hesperia and Apple Valley finally surpassed their older sister city in the number of homes built and population. Surveys had indicated that those who had purchased lots in Hesperia and Apple Valley during the 50s and 60s fully intended eventually to build homes on their lots there and reside permanently in the high desert. The fruition of these plans, in many cases, occurred soon after retirement from employment "down the hill." Subdividers continued to develop houses on relatively low-cost land appealing to first-time home buyers who still worked below Cajon Pass but were willing to commute to their own homes instead of paying rent and living closer to work. By early 1987, Hesperia had 10,678 single-family dwellings, Apple Valley had 8,986 and Victorville had 8,169. The 1990 census indicated Hesperia had become the most populous of the cluster of communities, with 49,000 residents and 4,000 more added the following year. Apple Valley's residents numbered 44,850 in the census and also gained almost 4,000 in 1991. Victorville was again gaining on her larger neighbors, up to 44,500 from 39,100 in 1990.

Victorville remained the commercial center of the burgeoning greater community. After already expanding the business district the entire length of Seventh Street, a substantial shopping area developed adjacent Palmdale Road across the freeway, centering on Gemco, which opened in 1982. But by that time, as the three towns touched each other at the edges, locations near Bear Valley Road and more central to all made much more sense. Thus the Mall of Victor Valley, a $40 million shopping complex developed just four years later, proved to be a brilliant economic move for the developers and retailers involved. Unfortunately, the transfer of longtime businesses such as JCPenney from old downtown Victorville and to a lesser extent, Sears from a more central location on Seventh Street, helped signal the decline of the earlier business centers for all but residents of the immediate vicinity. Besides the large mall, the neighboring Village Center and Victor Valley Home Center soon appeared on the frontage roads both sides of Interstate 15, just north of Bear Valley Road, each containing a considerable cluster of additional stores and other businesses. Expansion south and west of the main mall would soon follow. The Foxbourough Business Park, near the growing business center adjacent Bear Valley Road and Hesperia Road also housed an increasing number of new businesses and offices.

(Far right)
Postcard of Spring Valley Lake community view to the northeast

Mall of Victor Valley was one of the first in the region to feature a "food court," which proved to be popular and profitable.
Mojave Desert Magazine

The valley economic structure diversified considerably in the service and manufacturing sectors during the latter third of the century. California Interstate Telephone Company, incorporated in 1954, located general offices in Victorville and commenced dramatic expansion in the 1960s, including a complex of five buildings near Mojave Drive and Interstate 15. Continuing to acquire other small companies, it was purchased in July 1965 by Continental Telephone and much later merged with General Telephone. The increasingly complex computerized switching facilities remaining at the old location continued to generate a good deal of local employment. Housewife Coleen King parlayed assembly of electronic components on her kitchen table into King Hi-Tech, a $20 million business by 1984. Unfortunately, this operation could be more efficiently conducted closer to Silicon Valley and the company did not remain long in Victor Valley. A more permanent manufacturing plant, A.F.G. Industries, Inc., a giant glass works of 348,000 square feet, was established near an area long-zoned as an industrial center near Hesperia Road north of Bear Valley Road. The plant soon employed 260 people and produced 500 tons of glass per day, particularly for the greater Los Angeles market.

Another promising aspect of high desert development, tapped for years informally by promotional efforts in each Victor Valley city, was the influx of financially independent retired persons. The Tatum Green Tree project initially assumed that not all retired people desired to separate themselves entirely from a family-oriented environment, and thus promoters imposed no age restrictions on who could purchase houses in the developments. Later, Spring Valley Lake, developed by the western states giant corporation Boise Cascade, utilized the same concept in what was intended to be a gated community with considerable restrictions to ensure high-quality residences and eye appeal. The community featured an artificially created lake fed by several of the longtime flowing wells characteristic of the former Verde-Kalin Ranch area south of the Upper Mojave Narrows. After resolving some initial problems, these waterfront lots became extremely popular,

Adelanto City Hall, the most elaborate municipal building in Victor Valley, was built during a time of aggressive city promotion in the last two decades.
Mojave Desert Magazine

San Bernardino County
Fair 1993 "pig races"
"Shades of Victor Valley," Victorville Branch, San Bernardino County Library, Ida Jean Green Collection

increasing in price from $17,000 at the end of the 1970s to as high as $140,000 just 10 years later. The number of vacant lots continues to diminish as residence construction has persisted through good and poor economic times. Permanent residents far outnumber weekend visitors and there is an ever increasing proportion of younger families locating there. Silver Lakes, near Helendale, draws on a similar format and appeal. The old Jess Ranch, converted from turkey production to its origins as a guest ranch, features a retirement community with age restrictions still rare in the high desert, though common in many other communities.

The last decade of the century started badly so far as maintaining previous prosperity and expansion was concerned. The value of buildings erected in 1990 dropped some 40 percent from the level of the previous year. And by 1994 the number of single-family homes constructed was less than one-third of that in 1989. To a small extent some residential building activity shifted to Adelanto, whose population jumped from 8,250 in 1990 to 12,050 in 1993. There had been but 14 homes built there in 1989, but this increased to 121 in 1990, 487 in 1991 and 966 in 1992. Adelanto civic leaders were more aggressive than other communities in attracting new businesses to their developing industrial park. This was impressive in comparison with their neighbors, particularly Hesperia, which was losing such firms at the same time. Unfortunately, at that point George Air Force Base closure became a reality for the high desert region. There is no way to discount the negative impact of the loss of 7,000 area jobs related to disbanding the facility that had done so much to stimulate recent growth in the valley.

As Victor Valley's phenomenal expansion got under way, a few farsighted leaders considered the possibilities of a unified city with one municipal government and school district. As an unmentioned precedent, the Riverside County towns of Edgemont, Sunnymead and Moreno were just then successfully consolidating into the booming municipality of Moreno Valley. There were numerous practical obstacles to such a move, some voiced in 1974 by longtime Victorville city councilman and mayor Terry Caldwell, amidst reports of the Local Agency Formation Commission hearing considerations of Victorville's water district annexing Hesperia into its service area. As some

High Desert Mavericks has been a reasonably successful and popular minor league baseball franchise in Victor Valley.
Mojave Desert Magazine

feared this might be an "opening wedge" toward eventually annexing Hesperia, Caldwell assured them that Victorville did not wish to inherit the problems of its southern neighbor's undeveloped acreage and "substandard streets." There were continued discussions among some civic leaders in the early 1980s. More than a few acknowledged the efficiency of having one unified government and school district, including a bus system, instead of four or five similar entities each providing the same services, with their own expensive administrations and infrastructures.

The California Legislature had attempted to persuade school districts in neighboring communities to unify in the mid-1960s. At that time school officials sometimes conceded that such a move in Victor Valley appeared almost inevitable. But most elementary school board members and their supporters held firm for local control of their schools, with a unification vote defeated by a two to one majority in April 1965. The next year both Hesperia and Apple Valley requested that county officials investigate the feasibility of both cities forming their own separate unified districts, with most members of their communities continuing to favor that course until finally accomplished in the ensuing decades.

Largely stimulated by the adjacent booming George Air Force Base, Adelanto incorporated in 1972. Undoubtedly the dramatic growth experienced by both Apple Valley and Hesperia did much to spur both toward successful incorporation movements in 1988. This essentially doomed consideration of the greater unification effort, although some, including Caldwell, still conceded it had some merit in eliminating duplications in administrative functions. If prospects for one city were not already doomed, the bitter family fight over future control of the abandoned George Air Force Base facility ended any serious possibility of unification.

In 1996 Apple Valley Mayor Steve Wilson reviewed the subject in the realistic context of efficiency. But Adelanto Mayor Charlotte Foster countered with equal realism concerning local attitudes, observing that each community had its own identity, and questioned why that should be changed. Assemblyman Keith Olberg correctly explained that such a drastic idea would have to be carefully sold to the citizenry. A fiscal impact study would have to be conducted, reminiscent of what Victorville leaders did four decades earlier when considering incorporation. Simply comparing the relative costs of the unified and current fragmentized approaches might do much to overcome inertia and the firmly established parochialism surrounding the matter. But it would take much more to accomplish unification as a new city of Victor Valley.

Meanwhile, as the nationwide economic recession of the early 1990s continued, a number of major area businesses also closed. Some, such as Montgomery Ward and Service Merchandise, did so because of corporate downsizing. Hughes Market's merger with another grocery chain gave it two stores in rather close proximity, resulting in closure of the Bear Valley Road store. Kmart in Victorville closed due to lack of business, although companion facilities in Apple Valley and Hesperia remained open. The number of vacant commercial buildings throughout Victor Valley indicated not only previous over-expansion but continued economic stringency.

Yet as the turn toward the new century approached, there were substantial indications of recovery and continued growth. It turned out that in total employment levels, the valley never stopped expanding. Between 1991 and 1997 the number of people employed in Victor Valley increased from 30,523 to 39,192, despite the closure of George. The total area payroll increased from $304 million to $461 million annually. The area's proximity to the Southern California megalopolis, while still offering reasonable real estate prices along with good transportation linkages, naturally pointed to excellent possibilities as a distribution center. Rodeway Express trucking company, long-located near George Air Force Base, already understood and took advantage of this. Heilig-Meyers, a successor to the longtime California furniture dealer McMahan's, also recognized the situation and built a 471,000-square-foot warehouse-retail facility in Hesperia, adjacent to Interstate Highway 15, in 1997. Two years later Goodyear, the huge tire-manufacturing and retailing company, announced intent to construct a warehousing-distribution center almost twice that large, well under way in mid-2000. In fact the entire Southern California Logistics Airport, inheritor to much of the abandoned George Air Force Base facility, is based primarily on international shipping and redistribution from the Victor Valley to the greater far Western region. This appears to be one of the most promising aspects of the area's economic future.

The overall outlook for Victor Valley's approaching decade is indeed bright. Few communities can expect to double their population in a 10-year period of time, but that is a realistic prospect and challenge for the coming high-desert metropolis. Certainly there are many vacant areas interspersed within the existing homes of the valley. However, doubling the population will necessitate major housing expansion in all directions — through Lucerne Valley, beyond Phelan and El Mirage, toward Barstow and into Summit Valley, already projected for some 30,000 people. In such a situation, the high-rise buildings some have projected for more than a decade are not so far-fetched as they once seemed.

There have been many times when the governmental services and infrastructure, including roads, water systems and schools, could hardly keep up with the demands of the rapid expansion in Victor Valley. Yet residents have never suffered the really serious growing pains experienced by many in other places. Perhaps the persistent item of greatest negligence has been east-west highway planning and access. From the beginning of modern Apple Valley there has been talk of some highway entry corridor other than Main Street, Hesperia, Bear Valley Road, Seventh Street and Highway 18 through Victorville. This has never materialized, although the talk continues. Certainly with the insistence of perceptive citizens, this and other problems will continue to be resolved in a timely manner.

Numerous residents moved to the high desert to escape the crowding and pollution often experienced as metropolitan Southern California expanded. In a sense those problems came to the high desert with them. The implications of continued growth are both exciting and perplexing. As the burgeoning metropolis of Victor Valley continues to develop, the area will overcome whatever challenges arise, as the citizens of Victor Valley always have.

Partners in Victor Valley

Building a Greater Victor Valley

Business & Finance

Manufacturing & Distribution

Networks

Professional Services

Quality of Life

07824038 A
12
12

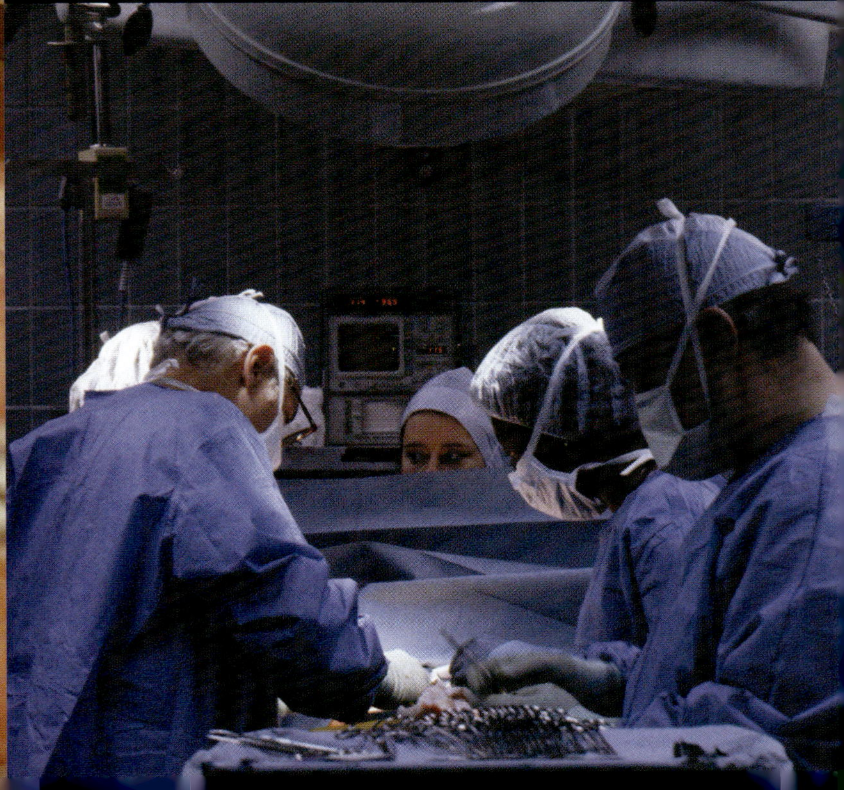

Southdown California Cement, LLC

Carl Leonardt, founder of Southdown California Cement's Victorville plant, was born in Westphalia, Germany, in 1855. He arrived in the United States in 1885 and quickly put to use his training in engineering and cement production as a salesman for the Dykeroff Cement Company of Weisbaden, Germany.

Carl Leonardt, founder of Southdown California Cement's Victorville plant

Recognizing the vast potential that cement manufacturing commanded as the United States grew by leaps and bounds, Leonardt was bound and determined to get in on the business. Leonardt realized his dream in 1907. In a partnership with Texas businessmen Felix Martinez and A. Courchesne, Leonardt incorporated the Southwestern Portland Cement Company. Subsequently, Southwestern Portland Cement opened its first cement-manufacturing plant in El Paso, Texas, in 1910.

With cement manufacturing successfully underway in El Paso, Leonardt tipped his hat in the direction of Southern California. Sometime around 1911 he relocated to Los Angeles. In Los Angeles, Leonardt prospered in his own right as a leading cement contractor. Innumerable projects around Southern California were built under the auspices of the Carl Leonardt Construction Company. Buildings such as the Hotel Green of Pasadena, the Bakersfield jail, Los Angeles Hall of Records and the American Beet Sugar Factory in Oxnard were stamped with the indelible quality of Leonardt's skillful construction.

Southern California of the early 1900s satisfied the promise of America's westward migration. Leonardt knew that with the progression of improved transportation —new railway lines and the newfangled automobile — throngs of people would come to California. And... with the people would come the need for roads, bridges, depots, factories, hospitals, schools and homes. Leonardt also knew that cement would be the material used to pave roads, bridge rivers and set the foundation for building cities. With the future in mind, Leonardt scoured Southern California for areas rich in the natural resources required for cement production. He found exactly what he wanted in Victorville.

The location Leonardt chose was on the banks of the Mojave River. It was an ideal spot because the river provided water for wet processing of cement and the land was rich in mineral resources, specifically, extensive limestone deposits just east of Quartzite Mountain. One sweltering August day in 1915, ground was broken for the construction of the Victorville plant.

An early photo of Southwestern's quarry operations and the company's train

On Labor Day of 1916, Southwestern Portland Cement's second and largest facility was put into operation. From the first shovel of dirt to the first cement-filled bag coming off the line, Leonardt supervised the plant's construction and operation. He even went so far as to build residential lodging nearby to guarantee his availability to oversee every detail regarding his pet project.

After completing the Victorville plant, Leonardt turned his attention toward America's heartland and the metropolitan explosion occurring in the Midwest. Southwestern Portland Cement decided that Ohio should be its Midwestern hub and set to groundbreaking in Osborn, now known as Fairborn. The Ohio plant began cement manufacturing in June 1925.

"Death claimed Carl Leonardt," reported a Los Angeles newspaper in February 1927. A 40-year resident of Southern California, Leonardt was hailed as the "pioneer builder of the West." In the cement-manufacturing industry Leonardt is an icon. In California he is remembered as the man who built the future from the material of which dream cities are realized — cement.

Throughout the years Southwestern Portland Cement continued to operate under the same high standards set by Carl Leonardt. By the late 1960s, larger companies were throwing speculative glances in Southwestern's direction. In 1970, the giant Southdown Corporation of Louisiana finessed the purchase of Southwestern's five plants in Victorville, Fairborn, El Paso, Odessa and Amarillo.

In spite of technological advances in the cement industry, cement is manufactured today very much the same way as it has been for decades. The primary material used to make cement is limestone. Depending on the type of cement desired, other raw materials such as clay, bauxite, shale, quartzite and iron ore are combined with limestone to achieve the final product. In all cases the entire cement-manufacturing process begins at the quarry.

At Southdown's Victorville plant raw material is blasted from the quarry and transported by 85-ton quarry trucks to the plant's rock crushers. Under the power of a 300-horsepower electric motor the limestone is crushed to the size of softballs. Next, the softball-sized rock is conveyed to the secondary crushing system, rendering the material to one inch or smaller in diameter. Then, limestone and the additional raw materials are stockpiled, ready for additional processing in the raw grinding system.

For the raw grinding process, raw materials are retrieved from stockpiles and proportioned to specific chemical formulas. In ball mills powered by 4,500-horsepower motors, the raw mixture is ground into fine powder called raw meal. The raw meal is conveyed to homogenizing silos where it is thoroughly blended in preparation for the next step: the burning process.

The burning process begins at the top of the preheater tower, where raw meal is pumped into the tower, allowing the meal to mix with hot kiln gases. At this point the meal is preheated from the introductory temperature of 200 degrees and rises to 1,650 degrees. The burning process advances as the meal enters the kiln and it is heated to 2,700 degrees, at which time a chemical reaction occurs that transforms the meal to clinker. As the clinker exits the kiln it is cooled to 150 degrees and is then transported to clinker storage. The clinker will later be reclaimed from storage to be mixed with gypsum (which controls the set-up time of the product) and other additives, and then sent to a finishing mill.

The company's logo from a bygone era as it appeared on cement bags

The process nears completion at a finishing mill where huge rotating cylinders employ steel "crusher" balls to break down the meal and its additives into a fine blend of cement. Finally — the last step! The cement is sent to storage silos and is kept there until the call for bulk shipping or sacking is heeded. The cement is ready to be combined with sand, gravel and water to make concrete — the material used to build houses and highways, bridges and buildings... and so much more.

Cement serves the building and construction industries in myriad ways. For each kind of project there is a specific kind of cement to satisfy that project's criteria. By modifying the basic limestone formula and adjusting the burn time,

Safety Follows Wisdom — the 1929 safety award presented to the company by the national Portland Cement Association

Southdown's Victorville plant can produce many different types of cement. Most of the cement that is manufactured is called Type II/V. Type II/V is used for the foundations of buildings, constructing highways and general all-purpose contracting.

Another type of cement is Type III. Type III is formulated to provide strength at an early set-up stage, allowing a project the advantage of a shorter setting time. Southdown also makes a variety of additional specialty cements, including Block, Plastic, and Class G cements.

Regardless of the type of cement manufactured, quality control is of the utmost concern. At Southdown, the production process is computerized from start to finish. From a central control room equipped with a bank of computers, monitors report every aspect of production. In a keystroke, controls can be adjusted to maintain appropriate material flows, pressures and temperatures.

Rivaling Southdown's concern for quality is the company's regard for safety. At Southdown Victorville, safety is a time-honored practice based on the motto: "Safety Follows Wisdom." It is this motto that graces an eight-foot-wide, six-foot-tall, 5,500-pound concrete monument that stands sentry at the plant's administration building. Designed in ornamental relief are figures of working men and an industrial wheel. The monument is actually the 1929 safety award trophy presented to the Victorville facility by the national Portland Cement Association. The awe-inspiring monument is a fitting tribute to the Victorville plant's penchant for safety that began several years before the monument was awarded.

The company's *Victor Sifter* magazines retrieved from a 1930 time capsule report efforts to research and employ safety procedures in an era when industry was generally ignorant of safety enforcement. Southdown Victorville was a leading force in the education of a safe-operation doctrine. The first issue of the *Victor Sifter*, dated April 1928, advised: "If we would be successful in a campaign of Safety First, we must know Safety, not only a passing hobby, but as a real live issue every minute of the day." Additionally, for numerous years prior to the magazine's campaign, the Victorville plant aggressively promoted first-aid education by sponsoring training and competitions.

The company's attention to employee welfare is underscored in policy and action in more ways than safety awareness alone. For instance, in 1928, when workers from the mechanical department expressed a desire to advance their knowledge of mathematics, a company administrator donated books for a plant library. Encouraged to pursue instruction, the Victor Plant Educational Committee was formed. A math teacher from the local college was hired, and the weekly class opened on February 28 with a charter enrollment of 25 employee-students.

Social responsibility to employees continued through the lean times and the war years, too. During the financial strap of the Great Depression payroll funds ran short. Company leadership opted to borrow funds in order to guarantee a paycheck for all employees. Then again, when times were tough during war years, the company kept good on its return-to-work guarantee to employees who fulfilled wartime military service. Additionally, each year of wartime service was credited to employment seniority.

Today, Southdown California Cement at Victorville exemplifies the profile of an industry giant that hasn't lost touch with its employees and the community at large. From sponsoring company picnics and holiday celebrations to scout troops and sport teams, and by offering employees up-to-the-minute modern benefits enhanced by an in-house camaraderie, Southdown Victorville is honoring its past while building a future.

In the beginning when Southdown's Victorville plant began operations in 1916, Victorville itself didn't exist as an incorporated city. The oasis of mineral wealth that dazzled Carl Leonardt's vision of the future was, to the average person, no more than an eyeful of abysmal desert. Squatters' shacks dotted the harsh landscape and kept company with a scant number of established homesteads. Wildlife the likes of coyotes and rattlesnakes outnumbered the human population.

Starting with just one kiln, one rock crusher, two mills, four silos and a company-built railroad, Leonardt not only bought into the cement-manufacturing business, he helped to finance the future of what would become the city of Victorville. Undeniably, as California and the United States grew in population, the need for cement increased. To keep pace with the demand, the plant expanded, hired more people and sponsored additional community-based interests, thereby enhancing the quality of life throughout the Victor Valley area. By the 1920s, Victor Valley was beginning to look like a piece of real estate that had residential potential.

By 1920 two kilns were operating and in 1923 that number expanded to four. Also that year, Leonardt began building what would become a landmark on the high desert — a 230-foot-high smokestack unlike anything the area had ever seen. The smokestack wasn't just unusual for its height. Its true uniqueness was in the way it was constructed — quite literally from the inside out!

Men on scaffolds worked from the interior of the stack pouring sections of reinforced concrete. As consecutive sections went up in height, so did the men on scaffolds. When the stack extended above head-height, a wooden staircase was installed to allow the crew to return to earth at day's end. After completion, the workmen who had peered out over the stack's 230-foot top nicknamed it the "Supreme Crow's Nest of the Countryside." Undoubtedly, the landmark was Leonardt's pride and joy for he had his initials "C.L." inscribed on it.

The year before his death, Leonardt built a fifth kiln. In the wake of his passing, the plant continued to grow. In 1949 a sixth kiln was up and running and 8,500 barrels of finished cement were produced on a daily basis. Also that year, a seven-year expansion period commenced. By 1953 the plant had nine wet-processing kilns, six raw mills, 10 finish mills, 30 silos, a new crushing system and a 15-mile extension of railroad line connecting the plant to the Black Mountain quarry site. A new administration complex made room for yet another aspect of company growth — additional office space for a growing number of employees.

Southwestern employees put their first-aid skills to the test at a regional competition in Los Angeles, c. 1920s. *John J. Anthony, retired Southdown employee whose father, Peter L. Anthony, was part of this team*

Carl Leonardt's smokestack

And then, the real excitement began in 1984 when Southdown finalized a $100-million, state-of-the-art modernization project that sent the Victorville facility over the top, producing a whopping 1.4 million tons of cement annually. The project was, in part, the result of a deal cut with the Humboldt-Wedag Company in 1982. The contract deal stipulated for Humboldt-Wedag to add an 800,000-ton-per-year precalcining-preheater kiln and a 4,500-horsepower raw mill at Southdown's Victorville Black Mountain site.

A modernization project of this magnitude required the tearing down of obsolete equipment and facilities to make room for new operations. Several major undertakings were implemented in preparation for the modernization project. These included abandoning kilns 5, 6 and 7 and leaving kilns 8 and 9 on standby status. Also marked for abandonment were six mills and an old packinghouse.

The modernization project was actually two projects in one that modernized both factions of the Victorville plant: the Black Mountain site and the Mojave River facility. Additionally,

The progress was phenomenal. To commemorate the plant's success, a second time capsule was prepared. A report taken from the 1953 time capsule echoed the employees' spirit of excitement in having unearthed the first time capsule. The message explained: "... so it comes to pass that some of us who witnessed the first ceremony are still at the cement plant, and rather than tottering down to view the last remains, some time in the years to come as we had anticipated, we place a new message in the second box while we are still enjoying the interesting developments of a Work-A-Day World bristling with activity and excitement."

From 1954 to 1980, improvements such as the 1959 implementation of the industry's first glass bag filter; the 1965 installation and operation of a new dry-processing kiln; a 1978 4,500-horsepower finishing grinding mill; and the 1980 installation of a new coal-handling and burning system kept Southdown Victorville at the top of the list in cement manufacturing.

a 4,500-horsepower finish mill and new clinker storage, along with new cement-packing facilities at the Mojave River site were part of the project. In accordance with air-quality standards, the new clinker storage was completely enclosed to reduce the chance of particles being released into the air. All in all, $20 million of the total modernization cost was invested in equipment that satisfied or exceeded air-quality regulations.

At Southdown Victorville, it's fair to say that air quality and emission control can be uttered in one breath. No less than 80 dust collectors are located throughout the facilities. Commonly called baghouses, the collectors use bags that collect 99.995 percent of the fine dust particles before the gases are released into the environment. An excellent example of the emission-control system is the largest collector located on a kiln exhaust. This particular baghouse uses 2,856 fiberglass bags - enough fiberglass material to cover six acres.

The Victorville plant emphasizes the fact that its greatest resource (by far) is its 250-plus employees. Employee jobs vary and include control room operators, mill operators, instrument, maintenance and mobile equipment mechanics, electricians, drillers and heavy equipment operators, administrators and office staff. Unconditionally, employees volunteer their skills for the welfare of the plant and the community at large by serving on councils and committees and giving unselfishly of their time and money to support local interests such as blood drives, hospitals and youth programs. With an annual payroll exceeding $13 million feeding into the community, Southdown is nourishing the growth of Victor Valley and laying the foundation for a promising future.

Unmatched in the industry for incorporating quality with progress, Southdown recently set into motion a $160 million expansion plan. Central to the project is a new pyroprocessing system, and additional high-efficiency raw material and finish grinding systems. These improvements revolve around implementing a technologically advanced precalciner system, additional raw grinding roll presses, a new 8,000-horsepower finish grinding system and two new high-capacity bulk loading systems. Upon expansion completion in early 2001, the Victorville plant's cement production capacity will increase to over 3.1 million tons per year, making it the largest cement plant in the United States.

Back in 1916, Carl Leonardt cast his eyes on the sun-scorched desert of Victor Valley and envisioned a future in the building and operation of a cement manufacturing plant - but he could not have imagined to what degree his dream would be realized. Today, Southdown's Victorville plant is a concrete testimonial to Leonardt's keen business sense and his far-reaching faith in what dreams may come when they're built on a cement foundation.

Together, these employees represent more than 400 years of Southwestern/Southdown work experience. (Left to right) back row — Eric Hug Jr. and Eric Hug Sr.; front row — Juan Martinez, Chuck Hattendorf, Shirley Davisson, Frida Monsanto, Doug MacIver, Lois McNeil, Mike Yannone, William Hug and John J. Anthony
Photo by Elizabeth Cox

The Bradco Companies

Southern California's real estate boom of the 1880s materialized by way of ballyhoo campaigns that promised farfetched investment returns. As opposed to a century ago, today it is a different story. Take for example the enterprising land development in Victor Valley. The taproot strategy of this boom is underwritten by logistical surveys, economic analysis, and population, labor and growth evaluation. Once all this data is studied it is utilized under the expertise of Joseph W. Brady, president and founder of The Bradco Companies, a commercial, industrial and land brokerage company in Victorville. At Bradco the illusions that plagued California's boom of yesteryear gave way to the winning side of integrity.

Bradco's integrity is underscored by a history dating back to a signature moment in Brady's life. An 11-year-old Brady was knocked off and under the back of a truck on his way to summer camp. Pinned under the truck's axle, his liver ruptured. Given a mere 3 percent chance to live, he pulled through with indomitable will and an indelible determination to make every moment in life count in a positive way whenever and wherever possible. His new found expectations were a tall order for anyone — anyone except Joseph Brady that is.

Deborah K. and Joseph W. Brady

He went on to graduate from California Polytechnic State University, San Luis Obispo, in 1979 with a degree in business administration enhanced by a concentration in business management and real estate. By 1980 he was president of the Santa Barbara Management Corporation, overseeing the business side of 980 apartment units. Brady spiraled upward into positions of greater responsibility. First with Islay Investments of Santa Barbara and then Sundesert Development Incorporated and on to the Pegasus Development Corporation, which was the gate-opener for Brady's move to Victor Valley.

Relocating to Victor Valley was a long-studied jump on opportunity that also proved to be the proverbial leap of faith for Brady. He had researched several California regions that held potential. Victorville won out because the area provided a canvas for the kind of person Brady is — an individual seeking a community where he could put down personal roots and develop the land to successfully serve the demands and needs of the population. Lock, stock and barrel he set out for Victorville on Friday the 13th of May in 1988. The ominous superstition of that fateful date did not escape him. Brady awoke the next morning wondering if he had made a mistake. In the eye of time, his query was no more than a blink. One good hard look around the landscape gave Brady his bearing and with an argus eye toward quality land development he put his sagacity and energy to work.

Brady incorporated The Bradco Companies in 1989, setting industry standards for offering full-service real estate brokerage packages. Bradco manages all aspects of brokering residential, commercial and industrial properties, and oversees joint ventures and land mitigation. The firm goes all out to put the right people together to compliment a project. This effort often involves connecting the talents of architects, engineers, marketing specialists, title administrators and interior designers to build a winning team. Brady also takes a higher step in spreading the good news to attract investors to the area.

(Far left)
Future site of The Victor Valley Promenade: a 32-acre retail development project adjacent to The Mall of Victor Valley
Courtesy Joe Zuccaro

Victor Valley's only four-story Class "A" office building is an example of properties represented by The Bradco Companies.
Courtesy Rob Kurth

His quarterly trade journal, *The Bradco High Desert Report,* sounds out 5,000 strong per issue. Heralded in the *Los Angeles Times* newspaper as a publication that discusses the general economic conditions of Victor Valley, including commercial, industrial and residential trends, Brady's *High Desert Report* is a billboard for attracting businesses and residential growth to the region.

Who are the people attracted to Victor Valley? Unlike the boom of 1880, people today move to the area for a different kind of promise. It's a promise that fulfills the reality of living, working and investing in a life far away from smog-encrusted cities jammed with traffic and riddled with crime. Today, opportunity for land development goes hand in hand with the opportunity for lifestyle enrichment — these are the very principles upon which Joseph Brady operates his business transactions and conducts his personal life.

Moving to Victorville proved to be a second enlightenment for Brady — he found stellar success in his career *and* he got lucky in love, too. The old adage about not mixing business with pleasure doesn't ring true for Brady. He didn't just mix business with pleasure — he married them together. In 1997, Brady married his own vice president. Today Joseph W. and Deborah K. Brady have established Bradco as a premier commercial, industrial and land brokerage company.

Being a business leader requires phenomenal commitment to providing exemplary services from every angle. One example of Bradco's dedication is its affiliation with the American Industrial Real Estate Association (AIR). Los Angeles County-based AIR offers select brokers the exclusive service advantage of a multiple listing database of properties throughout Southern California. The AIR affiliation allows Bradco another avenue for marketing clients' properties. Besides staying abreast of the latest technology to promote and market customers' properties, Brady continually seeks to expand his education within the industry. Specific to his goals is his current enrollment in Certified Commercial Investment Management (CCIM) classes. Knowledge gained from these classes will enhance Brady's involvement in the commercial and industrial arena, allowing him to be on the cutting edge of the industry. As always, Brady maintains his priority of being relationship driven, putting clients' needs first as opposed to the traditional realty brokerage transaction of commission first and client second.

In considering the present and future needs of Victor Valley residents, Brady recently scored an exclusive agreement with International Franchise and Business Brokers of Pompano Beach, Florida, to offer franchises and distributorships to local entrepreneurs. The variety these franchises will offer allows consumers a greater choice in products and services ranging from apparel and household goods to recreational activities. This visionary approach to filling a void in the community is typical of Brady's strategy for creating harmony between business and lifestyle.

Success comes to people in different ways. As a boy Brady traveled down a camp road to encounter a close call with death. His harrowing experience was an awakening, setting into motion his determination to make every moment count toward the best hours in life.

But...what makes for success? In 1995 Brady was the first recipient of the Libertarian Achievement Award presented by the *Daily Press/Freedom* newspapers. Subsequently, in a 1996 interview Brady said: "Be involved in your community. Always tell your clients the truth and don't be afraid to take a firm position on issues you believe in." By all means... Joseph W. Brady lives and succeeds by his own words.

Mitsubishi Cement Corporation

When people drive on freeways in the Inland Empire, they are most likely driving on cement from the Mitsubishi Cement Corporation. These same people will also see dotted along the highways industrial buildings, shopping malls and houses that have been built with this same high-quality cement. Mitsubishi cement is widely used throughout Southern California, Southern Nevada and Arizona.

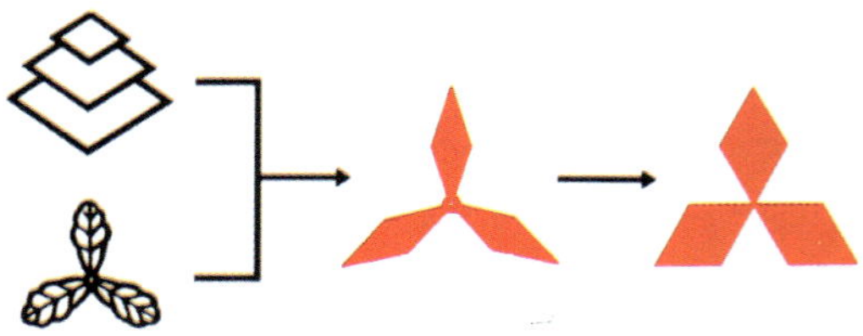

Yataro Iwasaki, the founder of the first Mitsubishi company, created the now-famous three-diamond mark by combining two images. He blended the angular forms of his own family's crest (top left) with the three-leaf crest of the Tosa clan, his first employer.

The Mitsubishi companies trace their history back to 1870 when Yataro Iwasaki established a shipping company founded with three obsolete steamships, traveling from island to island in Japan, transferring goods from seaport to seaport. The Mitsubishi name translates from the Japanese words "mitsu" meaning three, and "bishi" meaning diamonds. The Mitsubishi symbol originated in the flag mark of the founding shipping company and by 1910 had evolved into the red three-diamond trademark so well known throughout the world today. This small shipping company grew and branched into mining and shipbuilding. Iwasaki's successors expanded the organization further into heavy industry, chemicals, oil refining, aircraft production, banking, real estate, consumer products and insurance.

Following World War II, Mitsubishi was broken up into many independent companies. The individual companies went their own ways and now each company is publicly owned and traded on the Tokyo stock exchange. The only element still shared of the original conglomerate is the name, Mitsubishi, and its three-diamond trademark.

Mitsubishi Cement Corporation, USA, is currently owned by four Japanese companies: Mitsubishi Materials Corporation, Mitsubishi Corporation, Mitsubishi Trust and Banking Corporation and The Bank of Tokyo-Mitsubishi, Ltd. Mitsubishi Materials Corporation is one of the major manufacturers of nonferrous metals and cement in Japan, and Mitsubishi Corporation is the world's largest trading company. Mitsubishi Cement Corporation was formed in early 1988 when these four companies bought the assets of Kaiser Cement Corporation's Cushenbury cement plant, located in the Lucerne Valley, from Hanson, PLC.

The Mitsubishi Cement plant in the Lucerne Valley.

Because cement is manufactured from limestone, it is essential that the production plant be close to a limestone deposit. Mitsubishi's plant site is located in Lucerne Valley, adjacent to the quarry where the limestone is mined. The limestone is ground into the consistency of fine face powder, and then burned at a very high temperature of 2,700 degrees Fahrenheit. This process forms "clinker," which is almost like glass, and then is reground with various percentages of gypsum to a precise fineness, depending on the type of cement being produced.

The plant's work force of approximately 200 employees is responsible for mining the limestone and processing the raw materials in an enormous rotary kiln, which is operated 24 hours a day. The rotary kiln at Cushenbury is approximately 16 feet in diameter and 250 feet long, turning at about three revolutions per minute. It is the largest production single-kiln plant in the United States and has a rated capacity of more than 1.7 million tons a year of cement.

"Cement is often confused with concrete," explains one of Mitsubishi's employees. "Concrete is what you see in floors, driveways, highways, bridges, dams, and so forth. Concrete is a mixture of cement, rock, sand, water and other additives. When cement is mixed with water, it forms a completely different compound. Also, a concrete plant might cost around $1 million to build, whereas a cement plant could cost 200 times that amount."

Most of the company's cement goes into concrete and the rest is sold to various types of building material companies. In some cases, Mitsubishi sells cement directly, such as to the contractor responsible for the new Ontario Airport. In this project Mitsubishi cement was used for runways, taxiways and aprons for parking airplanes.

The management team and sales force of the company are headquartered in Ontario, which was chosen for the convenience of the Ontario Airport and close proximity to its major customers.

Over the last 10 years, Mitsubishi Cement Corporation has grown through a process of vertical integration, primarily within the downstream area of ready-mix concrete and aggregates. Mitsubishi has formed partnerships with the region's largest and most reputable ready-mix concrete and aggregate producers: Robertson's Ready Mix, located in the Inland Empire and the Los Angeles basin, and Superior Ready Mix, located in San Diego and Palm Springs. Mitsubishi owns 100 percent of the largest ready-mix concrete and aggregate producer in Las Vegas, Nevada Ready Mix. It also wholly owns Service Rock Products Company, a concrete and aggregate company in the high desert. In partnership with Lucky Cement of Taiwan, it has a cement import terminal located in Long Beach in order to import cement from overseas when the market so requires. It also has Hawaiian Rock Products, which produces ready-mix concrete, aggregate, asphalt and other building materials in Guam, Saipan and Tinian.

Mitsubishi Cement Corporation, as a Mitsubishi company, shares in the group's worldwide reputation for invaluable service to the public, strong future orientation, hard work for customer satisfaction, commitment to protect the environment and corporate reliability. Mitsubishi Cement Corporation, 12 years' strong, is proud to be a part of the history of the high desert.

The cement plant takes on an element of glamour in the night.

TXI Riverside Cement Company at Oro Grande

When Mrs. E.M. Potts arrived in limestone-rich Oro Grande in the early 1900s, she wasted no time putting her ambition into action. Potts untied her bonnet, rolled up her sleeves and seized the opportunity at hand to carve out a future from limestone.

A native of England, Mrs. Potts resided in Southern California with her architect husband, whose interest was clearly defined by the region's real estate boom. Knowing that limestone is the key element in cement, and speculating that cement would be the material of choice to build the up-and-coming cities, Mr. and Mrs. Potts went into the cement-producing business.

Mrs. Potts was the entrepreneur in the venture. Using her British contacts she finessed a plan to back the business with British capital. Her campaign succeeded. In 1906 the Golden State Portland Cement Company was drafted, and in 1910 the first Bear Brand cement was produced. And so began the history of Texas Industries (TXI) Riverside Cement's Oro Grande plant.

Growth of the Golden State Portland Cement Company had its lean years. The British capital was never quite enough to allow for improvements in a timely manner. In the wake of her husband's death in 1913, Mrs. Potts sought to improve the business with the addition of a new kiln. But finances were scarce and she was forced to sell the new kiln to the Riverside Cement Company. In 1917 expansion was attempted once again — but to no avail. The second kiln was also sold to the Riverside Cement Company. Finally, in 1923 Potts met with success and was able to take delivery on a new kiln. That same year, Riverside Cement Company made an attractive offer to buy out Potts and her backers through an exchange of stock.

Under ownership of Riverside Cement Company, its Oro Grande facility prospered. The plant expanded from the original one kiln to seven kilns. An additional Shay locomotive was acquired to haul the increased loads of limestone. Expansions were implemented in the crushing department, finish mill, raw mill and packinghouse. The Oro Grande plant operated at full capacity until the financial crunch of the Great Depression burdened the industry nationally. In 1928 the Oro Grande facility was shut down.

Answering the call of the World War II war effort, the plant reopened by request of the War Production Board. It was also during the 1940s that a modernization plan was executed. New raw and finish mills were constructed along with a new crusher and the addition of raw storage silos. The plant's modernization was hallmarked by the leading-edge installation of three of the world's largest dry process kilns. By 1946 the modernization project had succeeded to the point that of all the plant's original equipment, only five kilns were still in operation.

TXI Riverside Cement's Oro Grande plant's kiln control room.

Progress continued during the 1950s as the need for building materials increased. During this decade eight new finish silos were built. Plans were executed for the addition of two more massive kilns and additional raw and finish equipment. A 15-megawatt heat-powered generating station was implemented in 1954. The phenomenal progress was measured in the combined annual clinker producing capacity of 1.2 million tons.

A contemporary view looking out from the plant's quarry crusher shows the power plant on the left and silos on the right.

Throughout the years Riverside Cement Company's penchant for progress and advancement in industry technology has made its mark as a desirable interest in the cement manufacturing business. In 1958 the company merged with Peerless of Detroit and Hercules of Philadelphia to form the American Cement Corporation (Amcord). In 1979 Gifford-Hill and Company acquired Amcord; and in 1986 Beazer PLC acquired Gifford-Hill. Continuing a few more steps up the ladder, in 1998 industry giant TXI took ownership. Under TXI, Riverside Cement can boast that it is one of the largest bagged cement producers in the United States. The Oro Grande plant alone manufactures 75 percent of Riverside's gray cement production total.

As a member of the California Cement Promotion Council, California Manufacturers Association, California Mining Association and the California Cement Manufacturers Environmental Consortium, Riverside Cement takes an active role in industry leadership.

Working with the state of California and local air quality management districts, TXI-Riverside Cement implemented the breakthrough technology of TXI's CemStar process for which TXI scored the 1999 United States Environmental Protection Agency's (EPA) Climate Protection Award. CemStar is a revolutionary process that has the potential to reduce worldwide carbon dioxide emissions by 90 million tons a year while at the same time significantly reducing oxides of nitrogen emissions from cement kilns.

The CemStar process is a dramatic example of TXI's corporate doctrine of using byproduct synergy to help the environment. CemStar not only reduces harmful greenhouse gases — gases that contribute to global warming — but increases cement production as well. It's an innovative recycling process that injects slag, a steel industry byproduct, into cement kilns.

The EPA recognizes CemStar as vital ammunition in the war against pollution. EPA official Kathleen Hogan had this to say about TXI's CemStar process: "We think it's a real milestone to have a significant reduction in greenhouse gas emissions with this new process. Cement production is a source of greenhouse gas emissions. TXI is certainly a leader in viewing opportunities to improve productivity as not only a way of enhancing the bottom line, but also as a way to help protect the environment."

This past year Riverside Cement implemented the CemStar process at its Oro Grande plant. Thanks to CemStar's stellar success, the Ore Grande plant is not only producing the cement that is needed to build the cities and highways of today — the facility is providing for a better future by taking part in protecting the environment of today, for tomorrow... and beyond.

Still standing: This vertical limestone kiln is a reminder of a bygone era when lime was manufactured on the Oro Grande plant site about 1884. Reportedly, by 1889 eight kilns were in operation, rendering a combined capacity of 950 barrels per day. Firewood transported by mule wagons from the Klondike area was used to fuel the kilns. Most likely this kiln was operated by the Union Lime Company, at least until 1902.

Cimarron Escrow, Inc.

As words go, "escrow" often prompts a person to shake their head in confusion. At Cimarron Escrow, Karen Moore and her staff are experts at demystifying the term. Simply stated, escrow is the legal engagement of an impartial third party in a real estate transaction. The escrow holder is the intermediary between buyer and seller that collects and remits funds as instructed. The basic concept of escrow is to safeguard both the buyer and seller during a property's transfer of ownership. It is also an escrow company's primary responsibility to oversee completion of all necessary instructions in the agreement. Typically, the escrow process includes, but is not limited to, ordering a title search, ensuring the completion of all legal documentation, closing escrow within time limitations, and disbursement of funds according to written instructions.

Located on Park Avenue in Victorville, Cimarron Escrow relocated to this new location in February 2000 to provide a more spacious environment for its staff and customers.

Whether buying a first home or investing in commercial real estate, having complete confidence in the escrow company is important. For this reason, Cimarron Escrow has been a leader in providing peace-of-mind services since 1987. In the everchanging world of real estate, Cimarron has withstood the test of time. Owner Karen Moore and her staff triumphed through the recession of the late 1980s and early 1990s when other escrow businesses fell victim to the economy. What is the key to Moore's achievement? Service — it is underwritten and unsurpassed in its integrity, knowledge, commitment and technology.

Escrow companies in California are classified as either controlled or licensed. While licensed companies are bound to the highest and most stringent regulations enforced by the California Department of Corporations, so-called controlled companies are not required to meet these same standards. As a licensed independent company, Cimarron provides a certificate program for its escrow officers, performs U.S. Department of Justice background checks on potential employees and prohibits employing anyone barred from the escrow industry. Additionally, Cimarron protects consumers' funds through its membership in the Escrow Agent's Fidelity Corporation, which provides fidelity coverage in the amount of $5 million in the event of theft of trust accounts.

Commitment to its consumers is yet another attribute that has made Cimarron first choice in the industry. To make technology serve her account holders' best interests, Moore spent 10 months in 1990 customizing a computer system before putting it into operation. The system is fully warranted under a maintenance contract and Cimarron performs nightly backups to keep operation at its highest standard. Moore's penchant for implementing technology to better serve the escrow business resulted in her company being the first of its kind in Victor Valley to produce computer-generated statements, disbursements and status reports. Furthermore, seeing the need to serve the public other than on a Monday-through-Friday schedule, Moore opened for business on Saturdays.

Cimarron's esteemed reputation was singled out in 1995 when the U.S. Department of Veterans Affairs awarded Moore an exclusive contract to perform escrow services on VA acquired property in Southern California's 11 counties. To this day, the contract is in effect and remains a point of pride with Karen Moore — who is still doing business as usual: undividedly dedicated to excellence.

Home Loan Mortgage Corporation

Following the founding of the United States and in the wake of continental exploration, private ownership of real estate became a countrywide concept. Then, amid the economic upheaval of the Great Depression, the idea of owning property evolved into the American Dream of home ownership available to all who are willing to work for it. Today, making the dreams of potential homeowners come true is the business of Home Loan Mortgage Company (HLMC) of Hesperia.

Employing a staff of over 100 Victor Valley residents, the company has assisted thousands of families in becoming homeowners.

For the vast majority of homeowners, purchasing a residence is made possible through a mortgage loan. A mortgage enables a person to buy property without having the funds to pay for it outright. Thus, more people can enjoy the benefits of homeownership. HLMC is a mortgage banking company with the power to close and fund mortgage loans in its own name, distinguishing HLMC from a mortgage broker. Employing a staff of over 100 Victor Valley residents, the company has assisted thousands of families in becoming homeowners. Amazingly, HLMC has accomplished this in less than three years since its opening in 1997. To what credit does the company owe its success? HLMC's stellar achievement is due to its founding partnership of five people: Mike Daniels, Robert Holliday, Paul Rozo, Craig Kelleher and Helen Young. Each is dedicated to turning the company's prosperity into the success of the home-buying public.

As a member of the California Association of Mortgage Bankers and the National Association of Mortgage Bankers, HLMC operates 40 branch offices throughout California, Nevada, Utah, Arizona, Illinois, Georgia, Colorado and South Carolina. In Hesperia where HLMC is headquartered, the company's concern for public well-being is a priority.

The partners and staff donate their time and money to over three dozen local causes ranging in spectrum from social service programs to youth sports and various religious organizations. Exemplary of the company's generosity is its recent sponsorship of the High Desert Habitat for Humanity. A bountiful $40,000 cash donation came directly out of the pockets of the five partners for the purpose of purchasing all the building materials needed to construct a home for a local family. Backing that donation was the hammer-and-sweat support of HLMC's staff who assisted in building the home. At the groundbreaking in February 1999 the employees aptly demonstrated what lending a helping hand is all about. Whether the job involved raising a wall frame or nailing a roof into place, they were there to get the project done. Their determination to finish the house resulted in the new owners, a family of seven, setting out the welcome mat at their new home 75 days later.

Home Loan Mortgage Corporation is changing the look of the landscape throughout Victor Valley, California, and elsewhere in the United States. It is a company with the expertise and vision to carve out the future and make the American Dream exactly what it is meant to be —the realty of owning your own home. As the saying goes... there is no place like home.

Home Loan Mortgage Corporation's staff outside the company's national headquarters in Hesperia

Sun Country Bank

Board of Directors:
Patricia K. Nickell, chair;
Charito V. Barter;
Joseph J. Camera;
Joseph D. Smith;
Gaetano M. Cicchini;
Dennis H. Guida Jr.;
Irving C. Lee;
Elizabeth I. Daily;
E. Lynn Caswell;
Henry B. Marvin;
and Michael T. Wilson,
president/chief executive officer.

Management:
E.W. Lemoine,
executive vice president/
chief financial officer and cashier;
and John L. Beck,
executive vice president/
chief credit officer.

The first commercial bank in the United States dates back to 1791 in Philadelphia. Since then, banks have invested in the future by providing the financial framework necessary to build cities. In this time-honored tradition, Sun Country Bank provides for Victor Valley's community by offering banking services vital to its growth.

Sun Country Bank's dedication to community success began in 1988 when several Victor Valley residents sought to answer the need for a locally owned and operated bank. In a unique change from customary administrative direction, the proposed board of directors represented the community at large and included a retired banker, a consultant-investor, a developer, six business owners and a teacher. An application for the bank was filed in March 1989. On September 17, 1990, after successfully selling $3.5 million in stock, Sun Country Bank opened its doors to the community.

Sun Country Bank's deposits and loans grew until the sharp edge of the recession slashed profits of financial institutions across the nation. Determined to survive the recession, Sun Country Bank revised its philosophy and changed its direction by hiring a second president and chief executive officer. The strategy worked. With additional capital, experienced bank personnel and a strengthened directorial board, Sun Country Bank rose above the recession to the benchmark goal of $100 million in assets.

Today, Sun Country Bank is an FDIC-insured institution and a member of the Federal Reserve System with offices in Apple Valley, Victorville, Lancaster, Upland, Mission Viejo and Laguna Niguel. The bank offers full-service banking that underscores personalized service to both commercial and consumer clients in and around the six communities it serves.

As a vital member of the community, the bank actively supports numerous organizations including Lions Clubs International, Rotary International and the Victor Valley Museum. Sun Country Bank also takes a leadership role in contributing to charities and individuals as needs arise. It has helped to sponsor the Human Race benefit the past few years and provides financial support to a wildlife pond adjacent to its founding office. Just recently, Sun Country Bank helped to teach elementary school children that pennies make good sense when it sponsored a penny drive to collect 1 million pennies!

Of particular interest regarding Sun Country Bank's community involvement is its work with Victor Valley's Future Farmers of America (FFA). The bank provides interest-free loans to FFA students for the purpose of buying and raising farm animals to be sold for profit at the annual San Bernardino County Fair. This unique and worthwhile program includes a checking account for each student and the added incentive that a small contribution is awarded back to each student who maintains good financial records and provides the bank with a photograph of their FFA animal.

From its inception to the present, and looking to the years ahead, Sun Country Bank is proud to be a valued member of the communities it serves.

Teeming once again with wildlife, Ole' Weepin' Willer Pond is a sanctuary supported by Sun Country Bank.

Mobile Pipe Wrappers & Coaters

Oil to heat homes, gas for cooking, water for drinking and gasoline for fuel — all are made available by way of pipelines. Because great quantities of expensive and often harmful materials are transported by pipelines, it's crucial that pipe systems be constructed to prevent corrosion. Corrosion control is the sole concern at Mobile Pipe Wrappers & Coaters.

Founded in Irwindale in 1953 by Jewel Colvin, Mobile Pipe was purchased by George Stoddard in 1975. With a college background in aerospace engineering and mathematics, Mobile Pipe was the perfect investment for Stoddard, whose interest was in owning a business with the potential for future expansion. At the time the company had two employees, and then Stoddard's brother, Joe, joined the ranks. By 1990 Stoddard was ready to relocate and expand operations.

After considering various locales, including San Bernardino and Lucerne, Stoddard chose Adelanto because it had acreage to accommodate expansion in an industry-friendly environment. Stoddard moved Mobile Pipe to a 30-acre, million-dollar facility. Additionally, Stoddard invested more than $1 million to modernize equipment, bringing the company up to par with larger companies in the business. It was a dollar-wise expenditure that paid off handsomely, allowing Mobile Pipe to expand to 40 acres in 1998.

Today, Mobile Pipe is unique in that it specializes in the application of 22 types of coatings, while other pipe wrapping businesses are limited to just one or two types. Also, other companies limit themselves to either small or large diameter pipe, while Mobile Pipe accommodates pipe diameters from one-half inch to 144 inches. Mobile Pipe's wide range of products and services enables the company to work its corrosion control magic on a variety of projects.

It's no wonder that Mobile Pipe was the corrosion control specialist chosen to work on the high-profile pipeline projects for the Ontario International Airport expansion, the Los Angeles Department of Water and Power, the Metropolitan Water District of Los Angeles, the California Aquaduct tie-in, Southern California Edison, Southwest Gas in Victor Valley, and the Department of Water Resources, also in Victor Valley. At present, Mobile Pipe has plans underway to facilitate the application of cement lining for the water industry.

Mobile Pipe's commitment to quality and safety is rivaled in only one area — its commitment to the community. The company enthusiastically supports Little League baseball and youth soccer teams. Mobile Pipe also sponsors various programs of Adelanto's Police Department with special concern given to the program that purchases bicycle helmets for children.

George Stoddard,
Mobile Pipe's owner and president

Industry leaders George and Joe Stoddard look toward the future to meet the needs of the corrosion control process, which is intrinsic to the success of pipeline material transportation needed in the world today.

Cabo Yachts, Inc.

One usually thinks of ships and sand in opposition to each other. Take for instance the fate of the *Sirocco.* Constructed in Los Angeles in the 1850s for the Briggs Brothers Shipping Company, the *Sirocco* was built to ferry passengers and cargo across the Colorado River.

The Briggs brothers' idea was to transport their boat from Los Angeles east across the desert by way of muletrain. All went well until the crew was seized by a storm of gale-force winds fortified with waves of sand. Shipwrecked in a desert sea, men and mules abandoned ship.

A likely end for a tale of ships and sand? Perhaps, if this weren't Southern California, where people delight in the unusual and ships and sand can lead to success. Such is the case regarding the phenomenal success of yacht manufacturer Cabo Yachts, Inc., located in the high-desert community of Adelanto.

Cabo Yachts' state-of-the-art production facility occupies 145,000 square feet. The newest plant expansion of the 9-year-old company's Adelanto site will allow for the more efficient fabrication of larger yachts planned for the future.

The winning story of Cabo Yachts begins with company President Henry Mohrschladt. Fascinated with boats as a child, Mohrschladt sailed his first boat down a rain-swollen street gutter. Mohrschladt's captivation with boats followed through to adulthood. After majoring in economics at the University of California, Irvine, he turned his back on a Wharton Financial School fellowship in favor of setting his sites on the open sea. Instead of pursuing a career in finance, Mohrschladt took a minimum-wage job at an Orange County boatyard, and what seemed a questionable career decision turned out to be a wise step on a path leading to success.

At the boatyard Mohrschladt met Michael Howarth. Sharing a keen interest in boats and boating, the two men formed a partnership of mutual interest that led to the building of their first boat: a 25-foot, double-ended cruising sailboat. That first boat, built in Howarth's Anaheim garage, sold for $11,700 at the In-the-Water Boat Show at Newport Beach, California. The year was 1976, and it was a very good year for Mohrschladt and Howarth to launch their new boatbuilding business.

Hard work and a firm commitment to building boats of the highest quality earned the partners recognition in the fiercely competitive sailboat design and manufacturing industry. By 1988 demand for sailboats built by the team of Mohrschladt and Howarth skyrocketed to the point that the two could afford to turn their sites elsewhere. They sold their sailboat manufacturing business to a Singapore shipbuilder, allowing them to focus their innovative ideas on crafting custom-built sportfishing yachts — called sportfishers in the trade. From the concept that quality is premier to the foundation of design, crafting and manufacturing, Cabo Yachts emerged. In 1991 Cabo Yachts moved to the high-desert community of Adelanto. Once again...eyebrows were raised. A yachtbuilder in a desert? And once again, what seemed in opposition to success was actually a stepping stone to it.

In Adelanto there was room to expand in a business environment that encouraged new industry. From its five-acre, state-of-the-art facility the team set up shop to build customized sportfishers designed for people who demanded the best in quality and safety for high adventure on the open sea. That first year in Adelanto, Cabo Yachts launched the first in a line of outstanding sportfishers: the Cabo 35. The industry cheered. Accolades for the Cabo 35 poured in from all corners of the world. *Saltwater Sportsman* magazine raved about Cabo 35's "solid quality and attention to detail." And *Sport Fishing* proclaimed: "The new Cabo 35 is so extraordinary that you must see it and drive it to believe it."

What did Cabo do next? The Cabo team set to work crafting yet another spectacular sportfisher, and another, and another. The award-winning team at Cabo Yachts delivered six new sportfishers in 1992, progressing to a sales record of $1.4 million. By 1993 Cabo sales soared into the $4 million bracket and factory space expanded from 10,000 to 15,000 square feet. In addition to setting a sales record, 1993 hallmarked the year that the ownership team of Mohrschladt and Howarth invited Greg Bourque to join them. A sales representative for Mohrschladt and Howarth since 1985, Bourque bought into Cabo Yachts in June 1993. Today, as part owner and sales manager, Bourque oversees the domestic and international marketing of Cabo Yachts.

A new Cabo 35 model, called the Express, was introduced in early 1994. Featured on the cover of *Boating* magazine in June, the Cabo 35 Express was hailed as a sportfisher that handled rugged bluewater chores "as easily as a tuna bends a rod." With the debut of the Cabo 35 Express, Cabo Yachts now had two popular sportfisher models. By the close of 1994, Cabo Yachts' sales topped at 30 units with a revenue of $7 million.

Ever aware of industry trends, in 1995 Cabo Yachts manufactured a smaller version of its highly acclaimed Cabo 35 series: the Cabo 31 Express. Meticulously crafted by renowned designer Louis T. Codega, the 31 Express aptly answered the need for a shorter hull (31 feet) in a deep-sea fishing boat. With the success of its Cabo 35 models and the new Cabo 31 Express, Cabo Yachts enlarged its facility to 75,000 square feet.

In 1996 Cabo Yachts' sales surpassed all expectations, selling 68 units and reaching a revenue high of $15 million. Could the Cabo team break its own record? Yes. In 1997 total sales tipped the scale at 77 units and sales climbed to $19 million.

Cabo Yachts scored unparalleled attention in 1997. This was due in part to its new Cabo 45 Express receiving the prestigious "Boat of the Year" award from *Boating* magazine. The Cabo 45 Express answered the call for more amenities and more room, but with the same uncompromising quality as the smaller 35 models. Powered by twin Caterpillar 3196 diesel engines and sporting a custom-quality cabin appointed with designer fabrics and woods, the Cabo 45 Express offered the best of both worlds: high-powered craftsmanship in a luxury setting. As American beauties go — the Cabo 45 Express regally garnered the crown.

The founders of Cabo Yachts were recognized for the outstanding quality of their product when their boat company was listed among 100 firms in *Fortune* magazine for producing one of America's 100 best products.

Yet another factor to Cabo Yacht's 1997 success was its marketing campaign. Previously, the Cabo team had pursued the lucrative international market. Noting that Italy, France, Asia and the United Arab Emirates had an expressed desire for U.S.-built sportfishers, Cabo Yachts increased its marketing efforts overseas. In 1997, $3.8 million of Cabo Yachts' $19 million revenue sailed in from foreign shores.

Boat builders work on as many as 30 Cabo Yachts under construction in the main production building. Cabo has developed a work force composed of the area's best artisans. Mechanics, electricians, engineers, carpenters, machinists, welders and upholsterers are employed in the process of completing the world's best sportfishing boats.

The Cabo team made 1998 a groundbreaking year in more ways than one. The Cabo 47 Flybridge sportfisher rolled off the production line to the applause of 200 employees. Described as "elegant" and "top-of-the-line" in the industry, the Cabo 47 Flybridge set the theme for the Cabo team that year.

As top of the line, Cabo Yachts was top in the industry as well. Named as "Exporter of the Year" by the United States Small Business Administration, Cabo Yachts excelled over nominees from all 50 states as measured by six criteria:

1. Increased sales, profits, and/or growth of employment because of exporting;
2. Utilizing creative overseas marketing strategies;
3. Developing effective solutions to export-related problems;
4. Demonstrated encouragement of other small businesses to export;
5. Providing voluntary assistance to other small businesses entering the export market;
6. Demonstrated cooperation with other firms in the creation of export trading companies and/or introduction of unique trading relationships, products or services.

On June 2, 1998, the "Exporter of the Year" title was awarded to Cabo Yachts in a formal presentation at the National Winner Ceremony held at the Old Executive Office Building in Washington D.C. The gala occasion was presided over by United States Vice President Albert Gore, who personally complimented Cabo Yachts on its achievement.

The "Exporter of the Year" award was received by Cabo President Henry Mohrschladt, shown with U.S. Vice President Al Gore at the awards reception in Washington D.C.

Cabo Yachts also broke ground in a very real sense that year. With sales of $24 million the company set into motion a groundbreaking expansion of its Adelanto facility. In order to meet the demands of domestic and foreign markets, the Cabo team increased its factory by 55,000 square feet, thus expanding total plant size to 145,000 square feet and production capacity by 25 percent.

From its first national acclaim in 1988, when *Fortune* magazine proclaimed boats built by Mohrschladt and Howarth among the top 100 products of "What America Makes Best," to present-day recognition as a world leader in the designing and manufacturing of sportfishers, the team at Cabo Yachts has demonstrated unrivaled excellence in boat building. What's the key to Cabo Yachts' success? Quality.

At Cabo Yachts quality is the product of complex research and an unwavering commitment to build each and every boat to perfection in design, performance, safety and construction.

When Mohrschladt and Howarth first formed what would become Cabo Yachts, they extensively researched the market. Highly regarded manufacturers and potential buyers were surveyed for input. After opinions and preferences were studied and competitors and markets were targeted, the Cabo team set to work to build a product that would serve as an industry standard, exemplary of the ideal sportfishing yacht.

The company employs strict standards in all aspects of design and manufacturing. Dedicated to the standard that quality and safety are always foremost in production, Supervisor Stan Broadfoot sees to it that everything — from the engines to the smallest cabinet latches on each boat — is perfect or inspection approval is denied. Is Broadfoot's penchant for perfection extraordinary? Yes, but not the exception. Quite the contrary, Broadfoot's thoroughness is the rule in quality and safety at Cabo Yachts.

Each sportfisher is designed for comfort as well as performance and fishability and can be custom outfitted to a buyer's personal taste. A master state-

Three Cabo 35 Express Sportfishers ply the waters of Cape Cod Bay in Massachusetts. The Cabo Yachts line has become a favorite of serious offshore fishing enthusiasts nationwide.

room might feature an oversized double birth, a roomy cedar-lined closet and a full-length dressing mirror. On the practical side, a sportfisher's cockpit features two huge 60-by-16-inch insulated storage boxes equipped with pumps to eliminate the untidy mess of melting ice and debris. Other personalizations have included imported upholstery fabrics, brass appointments and specially designed entertainment centers — just to name a few. All the creature comforts of home are combined with the luxury accommodations of a fine hotel outfitted on the highest quality sportfishing yacht that money can buy.

What's on the drawing board at Cabo Yachts today? In a effort to encourage responsible sportfishing today and into the future, Cabo Yachts enthusiastically sponsors the Billfish Foundation. The Billfish Foundation is a conservation and research group that works with national marine fisheries monitoring breeding and promoting a catch-and-release program of billfish such as marlin and swordfish.

Additionally, the Cabo team just completed a 65,000-square-foot factory expansion. And in an ongoing concern to meet the needs of clients, Cabo has a Web site that allows an online factory tour and a place for enthusiasts to shop for apparel and accessories unique to the sportfishing lifestyle.

Be it a sportsman's dream, an adventurer's dream, an American dream... yachts designed and built by the Cabo Yachts team are dreams come true. With the singular objective to build the finest-quality, best-performing sportfishing boats in the world, Cabo Yachts has made boatbuilding a success in the unlikely environment of a sand-swept California desert.

Cabo Yachts worked to increase its global market share through aggressively promoting its yachts at international trade shows, such as the Tokyo, Genoa, and Puerto Vallarta shows, and through international media. The measure of its success was winning the Small Business Association's "Exporter of the Year" award in 1998.

Safeway Sign Company

"It's a sign of our times," is more than just an expression for the family-owned and operated Safeway Sign Company. It's a nostalgic look at the past that brought this company from a garage to a position as one of the nation's largest traffic sign manufacturers. It all began in 1948 with Forrest O. Moore, whose background in transportation led him into the manufacturing of signs for vehicle traffic and safety. By the mid-1950s Moore had landed the first annual highway sign contract with San Bernardino County. Moore then began working with the California Department of Transportation, known today as CalTrans.

One of the company's first street address signs produced in the late 1940s

Moore's son, David G. Moore, joined his father in the business and in the late 1950s he took over the company. By 1962 David had built an 8,000-square-foot facility in the city of Gardena, in order to keep up with growing business and recurring state contracts. David's son, Michael F. Moore, joined the company as a production assistant in the metal department. In 1977 David semiretired and his son, Michael, became the general manager. Daughter, Andrea Moore Gutierrez, took over as office manager, and son, David C., took the position of sales manager in the mid-1980s. Today the father, David G. Moore, sits as chairman of the board in the family corporation; the mother, Judith J. Moore, presides as president; Michael is CEO, while Andrea and David C. are vice presidents.

Employees from the Gardena plant show off signs they've made.

Once again, Safeway Sign Company made a leap in production and growth, but this time it included a relocation out of the Los Angeles area to Victor Valley, where the family chose Adelanto as the site for its new 60,000-square-foot manufacturing plant. The new facility was built in 1991. Adelanto was chosen because of its affordable land, both for business and housing. Other reasons included its central location, easy access to the interstate and its railroad and trucking routes that are a hub of the city, and the city's enthusiasm for the new business.

Of the company's total workload, 75 percent is for highway traffic and work zone safety, while the other 25 percent handles the commercial and industrial sectors. Safeway Sign Company has continually maintained all of the major CalTrans contracts. Highway and street signs include street name signs, interstates, speed and safety warnings, and numerous other highway work zone signs. Safeway also manufactures the fixtures that mount signs on the ground or overhead. Safeway's signs can be found throughout the western United States and Mexico. The company has also been involved in making special designs and signs for professional athletic teams, the Los Angeles Arts Festival and the Adelanto Grand Prix, to name a few.

While the Moores continue to utilize advancements in technology, they still recognize the importance of people. Safeway Sign Company employs more than 70 people who are key to producing quality work for each and every sign, and the company takes pride in a sales staff that treats people the way they would want to be treated. One of the greatest advancements in the technology of producing signs is the changeover from manual cutting to computer cutting and the benefit of computer graphics. The company's production capability is impressive — Safeway can manufacture signs as large as 60 feet by 12 feet, or as small as 3 inches by 3 inches; and for each design, it produces quantities from one to over 1 million signs.

The company's greatest achievement thus far, according to the Moore family, was building its own production plant. The family shares a gratitude for always having been in a position to handle new opportunities and take on new projects. Perseverance and dedication have kept this family-owned and -operated business going strong for more than 50 years. Unwavering service and consistently high-quality products have won the company long-term contracts and repeat customers.

Inside Safeway Sign Company, a variety of operations are performed by state-of-the-art equipment. Computers aid in graphic design and laminating machines work at a constant pace, while metal fabrication, powder coating, welding and assembly are all taking place. Some of the letters are drilled by hand, one by one, and the reflective tape is hand-placed on each sign. Many signs are silk-screened with transparent ink in order to give the sign greater visibility. Reflective letters are also placed by hand on freeway signs. This well-designed harmony of worker and machine produces an average of 16,000 signs each week.

Safeway Sign Company is a member of the Adelanto Chamber of Commerce and has been a supporter of the Adelanto Grand Prix. Andrea serves on the Mojave Historical Society, while Michael is on the board of directors for the California Traffic Safety Service Association (CAL-ATSSA). The company is also a member of the American Traffic Safety Service Association (ATSSA).

With great pride and satisfaction, the Moore family often reflects on how this business began, and it always leads them back to their grandfather and father who instilled in them values of integrity, hard work, pride, common sense and the importance of a smile. Looking to the future, the Moores plan on improving what works — and what has worked. There's no need to change this family's pattern for success as it continues to produce the "signs of life."

Para-Chem

Sometimes it is what isn't seen that counts. Para-Chem's chemical products, though usually invisible, touch the lives of millions of people around the world. Many industries, from carpets to airlines, rely on its adhesives, polymers, thickeners, coatings and specialty chemicals to enhance the appearance and performance of their products.

Para-Chem manufactures its chemical products in Victor Valley and at four other U.S. facilities. Since it began making latex coatings in 1952, Para-Chem has enjoyed continued growth. Privately held and operated by the Jordan family, the company is headquartered in Simpsonville, South Carolina. President John W. Jordan III maintains the same quality philosophy and environmentally friendly products that have earned the ISO 9001 company its reputation for excellence.

Through the years, Para-Chem has added new adhesives, thickeners, coatings and surfactants to its ever-expanding product line. "Our success comes from giving our customers the best value for their dollar, putting quality first and conducting our business with the highest ethical standards," Jordan says. "Para-Chem's strength as a company is the ability to make custom formulations that meet customers' unique needs."

An experienced team of chemists and technicians develops new products with state-of-the-art technology. All products are tested hundreds of times to ensure consistent high quality from batch to batch, and from year to year. A pioneer in the development of low-VOC chemicals, the company has created a line of solvent-free products that are both environmentally friendly and safe for the people who use them every day.

Para-Chem's service team offers individual attention and problem solving, and a fleet of company-owned "Rapid Response" trucks delivers products from the company's plants. Customer service representatives ensure that orders are delivered on time to exact specifications, and technical service coordinators follow up with answers to customers' questions. Because of Para-Chem's dedication to building long-term relationships, several large, well-known companies, including Masland, Hoechst Celanese and Culp Inc., have honored it with Supplier of the Year awards.

Products

Para-Chem's fast-growing polymer division serves companies in the textiles, graphic arts, roofing and paper markets, to name just a few. Para-Chem polymers add strength and durability to a wide array of products, from leather and vinyl finishes to carpets and printing inks. Its polymers can be made to resist water and solvents or to improve flexibility. Para-Chem pioneered the development of environmentally safe, fire-retardant polymers that are so important to home and commercial textiles.

Para-Chem's specialty coatings are used in everything from upholstery and weather-resistant fabrics to aircraft textiles. Employees in this growing division bring nearly 300 years of collective experience to the task of developing custom coatings that make products more durable, attractive and fire-resistant.

The Para-Chem facility in Adelanto, California

In the floorcovering business, Para-Chem is famous for its PARABOND label products. Long popular with professionals, these adhesives are now available to homebuilders and the do-it-yourself market. In Adelanto, Para-Chem makes cement patch and underlayment products under the VITEX label, as well as a complete line of NOVATEX floor care cleaners, spot removers and odor eliminators.

Para-Chem technology is just about everywhere — in homes, at work and at play. Although the products are sometimes hard to see, Para-Chem is making a big difference in people's lives!

Hodhod, Inc.

Self-employed since 1980, Eddie Hodhod set his sights on building a future and traveled the road of opportunity to Victor Valley. There, near one of California's busiest corridors, Hodhod went into business as the owner-operator of a gasoline service station alongside Interstate 15. A mere six years later he established a car rental agency adjacent to the commercial hub of Victorville on Palmdale Road.

The anchor service of Thrifty Car Rental was enhanced to provide rental of the nationally recognized Ryder trucks.

Having made a home for himself in the high desert, Hodhod is today the owner and president of Hodhod, Incorporated, a multifaceted company dedicated to meeting the motoring needs of the area's residents and visitors. Hodhod's success is certainly a credit to his business savvy and service-oriented attitude of staying on top of the needs and requirements of the entire community.

In order to accommodate the ever-expanding needs of the region, Hodhod increased his offerings of in-demand services. The anchor service of Thrifty Car Rental was enhanced to provide rental of the nationally recognized Ryder trucks. Additionally, for the convenience of vehicle owners, he runs a California state smog certification and auto repair facility. All of these services are located under one roof and are skillfully managed by Sandy Hanson. As if vehicle rentals and auto repair were not enough, Hodhod recently included apartment rentals to his ventures to accommodate local businesses' needs for short- and long-term relocation services. As for future plans, he is keenly aware of the vast potential of the vacation and recreational vehicle market. Currently he anticipates adding motor home rentals to his agenda.

High spirited about the region's future, Hodhod explains that "the Victor Valley area is important to me because I feel I have grown with the area. The valley has been very good to me." He is not shy in the least about acknowledging the fact that Victorville afforded him the chance to satisfy his ambition as an individual and entrepreneur. In appreciation he and his employees generously support local organizations and charitable causes. His sincerity in fostering an overall well-being in the community is starkly apparent in the choice of sponsorships. Children benefit from Hodhod's advocacy of the Victor Valley Christian School and the local 4-H Club. Additionally, St. Anthony's Monastery and the substance abuse program of the California Narcotics Association are recipients of his attention.

Hodhod originally sought out Victor Valley because he was looking to put down roots in a town that would allow him to make a living pursuing his ambitions rather than working for someone else. Now, having attained the goals he set to achieve, he could easily move on. He chooses not to, however. It is evident by the look in his eyes that Victor Valley holds untapped potential that Hodhod will not let go undiscovered. After all, this is the community with which he has prospered and he has every intention of contributing to its future.

An expanded rental fleet allows Thrifty to provide an array of vehicles to customers at a moment's notice.

Responsive Internet Systems, Inc.

Good communication is often one of the keys to success. Responsive Internet Systems, Inc. (RIS) has unlocked this key, and thus it has doubled in size every year since its inception in Apple Valley in April 1995. RIS provides communications construction and service and complete infrastructure improvements and telecommunications. It emphasizes excellence in this fast-moving world of communications.

PUBLIC WORKS, SCHOOL DISTRICTS AND MILITARY BASES HAVE PROVIDED A STRONG REPEAT CUSTOMER BASE FOR RIS, AN AMP NETCONNECT DESIGN & INSTALLER (NDI) CONTRACTOR.

Sole owner and President Kevin W. Squire had 12 years of experience in electronics and an intense, growing interest in telecommunications when he decided to found RIS. He began in his home, and in just one short year he had doubled his volume and had to lease a building to house his rapidly growing business. In each of the next two years, RIS again doubled in size and volume. Squire realized that he had to make the transformation from a "mom-and-pop shop" to a corporation that would meet the future with no restraints.

Squire developed and wrote an outstanding business plan for the growth and future of RIS, which earned the business a Federal Redevelopment Grant. This grant enabled Squire to improve the industrial business facility he purchased for the relocation of RIS to Nomwaket Road in Apple Valley.

RIS is unique in that it performs all aspects of the set up of a communications operation. The company employs backhoe operators for the trenching needed to lay fiber optic cables, as well as telephone technicians, electricians, computer programmers, project managers and key office staff — more than 60 employees in all. Squire believes that the company's niche in the communications industry is the fact that RIS is a full-service company. Additionally, doing all work in-house has enabled the company to be very competitive. Most important are the company's commitment to quality and a work ethic that has proven itself time and time again — that all jobs will be completed to customer satisfaction.

Public works, school districts and military bases have provided a strong repeat customer base for RIS, an AMP Netconnect Design & Installer (NDI) Contractor.

The business facility of Responsive Internet Systems, Inc., located on Nomwaket Road in Apple Valley

RIS has handled projects of all sizes, from wiring and cabling to linking schools within a district, and between districts. One of the company's largest jobs in Victor Valley was for the Silver Valley Unified School District, which included the district office and six school sites. The schools had virtually no wiring with which to begin, and when RIS completed the project, the district was connected by a state-of-the-art network. RIS's largest job to date was for the Fontana Unified School District, setting up a complete network for 33 sites. Thirty of these sites were existing schools and required a tremendous amount of trenching and cabling. The other two sites were existing newer schools.

RIS Owner and President Kevin W. Squire

RIS has also serviced numerous colleges and universities in the San Bernardino, Riverside and Orange counties.

Work at the area's military base has also been an exciting experience. In 1997 RIS won the contract to run all the fiber optics for the largest-ever electronic warfare practice at Fort Irwin. A T-3 line, a 45-megabit phone line, was installed that connected Congress in Washington D.C. to 450 generals directing tanks and troops wearing helmets, both outfitted with computers, during simulated warfare. Watching a huge screen, the generals were able to see where their pieces of equipment were at all times.

RIS DONATED AN ENTIRE NETWORK TO A LOCAL CHRISTIAN SCHOOL AND IS VERY PLEASED TO HAVE BEEN ABLE TO PROVIDE A COMMUNICATIONS SYSTEM THAT THE SCHOOL MAY NEVER HAVE BEEN ABLE TO AFFORD.

Although RIS has secured most of its contracts in public works, Squire knows that continued success depends on its expansion into the private sector. RIS plans to remain strong in public works, especially in the field of education, but realizes that it is vital to become well known in private industries, such as medicine and banking. Squire sees a lot of work out there and his goal is to make sure that RIS is prepared to service all future anticipated business with the same quality control that has enabled the company to handle projects and contracts of all sizes.

The communications market is still young and Squire believes that newcomers may not have the quality necessary to survive. Loyal customers of RIS do not seem to shop. This may be due in part to the company's philosophy of rarely charging for change orders. RIS believes customer service is for the long term rather than the short term.

RIS is a member of the Apple Valley Chamber of Commerce and views community involvement as an important link in communications. RIS donated an entire network to a local Christian school and is very pleased to have been able to provide a communications system that the school may never have been able to afford.

Squire chose Apple Valley for his business location because of its affordable living and healthy climate. Though a highly driven businessman, Squire sees himself first as a family man, a husband and father of four sons.

Ninety percent of RIS customers are within a 90-minute drive from the company's base; however, expansion of its service area is definitely in the plans for the future. In a world where faster is better, RIS views the ever-changing computer industry as its greatest ally. The processor speed of PCs is continually increasing, creating a constant demand for system upgrades, cabling and electronics — all in a day's work for RIS.

Century 21 Fairway Realty, Inc.

Charlotte Phillips is an astonishing person. In the wake of her husband's — U.S. Air Force Maj. James Phillips — sudden death, she summoned every ounce of her determination and gathered all her resources to start a business that would support her family and provide a future for her children. As a mother and entrepreneur, Phillips became the cornerstone of what would become Century 21 Fairway Realty.

Charlotte and James Phillips were high school sweethearts from the Midwest. They married in Yuma, Arizona, and then traveled to Victor Valley when James was assigned to duty at George Air Force Base near Adelanto. While on a training mission in 1968, Phillips, a fighter pilot, was killed in an in-flight accident in Florida.

(Far right) Charlotte Phillips

Janie Phillips and Jim Phillips

For the sake of her children, Charlotte Phillips looked toward the future and the prospect of opening her own real estate business. Friends and family encouraged her. They had witnessed her uncommon success as a representative for Mary Kay Cosmetics and they knew she could transfer her keen business sense over to the world of buying and selling properties. After studying real estate and garnering the partnership of several retired military officers, Charlotte Phillips set her realty and business licenses on display and opened the doors to her new venture.

Year by year and one by one, Phillips bought out her partners. By the late 1980s, as sole owner, Phillips retired — so to speak — and transferred the business to her son, Jim Phillips, and her daughter, Janie Phillips.

Jim Phillips and Janie Phillips are both certified residential broker designees dedicated to upholding their mother's commitment to superior ethics, professionalism and personal service. Since the family-owned-and-operated company's first transaction in 1964, the business has grown with the region. Today they offer their Century 21 Fairway Realty customers the insight and expertise of over 60 agents who know Victor Valley as their own community.

Practicing a philosophy that every real estate transaction provides the opportunity to establish each new client as a customer for life, it is easy to see why the Phillips' team has earned the real estate industry's acclaimed Quality Service Award in 1993, 1994, 1996, 1997 and 1998. While buying and selling properties is still the core transaction in realty, the team also provides a broad range of services to meet the needs of the community and real estate industry.

In the Residential Sales and Marketing Department, associates are trained to negotiate and oversee every detail of a sale with the client's interest as their premier concern. In order to accomplish this, many aspects of the process are put into play including: market analysis, net sheet calculations, multiple listing service, advertising and promoting, contract negotiation, completion and signage services, property protection services, loan qualification assistance, selection assistance and arrangement of required inspections.

The Real Estate Owned Marketing Department team has provided service to lending institutions for over 15 years. This service is a vital aspect for transactions involving bank-owned properties and includes regular inspections, follow-up on repairs, providing utilities for inspections and updates on market activity and results.

The Century 21 Fairway team in Commercial Sales and Leasing specializes in soothing the growing pains of the Victor Valley community. By providing such services as investment analysis of income property, lease/management and leaseback agreements, sales and exchange

Century 21 Fairway Realty, Apple Valley

assistance, finance options, and access to a worldwide network used for inventory and marketing, the business supports the commercial and residential growth of Victor Valley.

Janie Phillips heads the training and Jim Phillips, the recruiting. The firm offers a full agenda of courses for the real estate professional as well as a series of classes that focuses on real estate basics. The classes are open to all qualified candidates along with a mentor program geared to assist the new real estate professional in getting off to a proper start. The team's dedication to ethical professionalism is no where more apparent than in these training sessions that set the exemplary standard of excellence for which Century 21 Fairway is known.

Century 21 Fairway Realty also handles all aspects of property management. Whether a property owner needs full management or simple leasing services, the Property Management Department handles it all from rental collection and staffing to tenant screening and background checks.

Relocation and referral services are also benefits the team offers to the community. With over 6,000 offices worldwide, Fairway Realty can take a lot of the worry out of a client's relocation concerns. Along these lines, two relocation and referral directors assist clients and transferees with vital information about the Victor Valley region or areas elsewhere in the world to which they are considering moving. Relocation and referral services are available to individual clients as well as the corporate sector.

The Phillips' sense of community spirit is apparent in the company's numerous sponsorships. As the Happy Trails Gang, Fairway realtors, associates, family and friends made a collective run of 131 miles in a 24-hour period to help raise $345,000 for the Easter Seals Society. In another high-spirited activity, Janie Phillips found herself behind jail bars in the March Of Dimes Birth Defects Foundation's Jail and Bail fund-raiser! The Phillips' team also supports Optimist International, St. Mary's Foundation, the Mojave Special Olympics and numerous community organizations.

What is on the horizon for real estate? Jim Phillips is quick to point out that realty companies will most likely provide one-stop shopping, including lending and title services as part of the real-estate package. To be sure, Century 21 Fairway Realty has its sites set on the horizon ready to meet the needs of Victor Valley's community.

Century 21 Fairway Realty, Victorville

Comarco Staffing, Inc.

Ever since the American industrial revolution of the 1800s business activity has progressed with population growth — taking the need for personnel services with it. Employment services today face the challenge of linking employee skills to business needs in continuously expanding markets. At Comarco Staffing, ladder rungs are set higher to match qualified employees with individualized requirements of Victor Valley employers.

Since its founding, Comarco Staffing of Victorville has answered employers' needs throughout a decade of record growth.

Founded in 1989 by Robert A. Lovingood as Hi Desert Personnel Services, the highly successful agency was purchased by Comarco Inc. in 1996. Lovingood continued with the company as president of Comarco Staffing, Inc. and vice president of Comarco Inc. Under Lovingood's visionary direction the business has grown into a multimillion-dollar company providing complete employer support services.

Recognizing employers' requirements vary, Comarco provides personnel placement across the board in the fields of technology, industry, secretarial, engineering, administration and management. The company's primary focus of providing short- and long-term employees is upheld by the integrity of its support services. These background services include substance abuse testing and policy implementation, professional recruitment, workers' compensation claims management and payroll services.

Employers are notably concerned about securing a drug-free working environment. Comarco alleviates employers' worries with a substance abuse program that enforces drug screening and education. By practicing awareness training and an employee assistance program, Comarco works with employers to create healthy working environments.

Recruitment services are the specialty of the company's professional recruitment division. This unique approach is ideal for companies requiring prequalified candidates and for businesses that do not have the time and/or resources to satisfy these needs on their own. A Comarco professional recruiter works directly with the employer to customize a profile of the perfect employee. Criteria such as education and training, experience and personality are fashioned into the profile in accordance with an employer's specifications. Filling a company's personnel vacancy in this manner is cost effective and results in a superior match between employer and employee.

Comarco Staffing is also a leading informational resource in the industry. Its tri-annual newsletter, *The Employer,* distributes nearly 2,000 copies with each publication. A recent issue discussed rate increases in workers' compensation, clarified legalities concerning interview questions and highlighted trade news including business profiles and community-based sponsorship of fund-raisers and charitable organizations.

At Comarco Staffing, ladder rungs are set higher to match qualified employees with individualized requirements of Victor Valley employers.

True to Robert Lovingood's philosophy of giving back to the community, he and the personnel at Comarco Staffing enthusiastically participate in myriad organizations including: Desert Communities United Way, Lewis Center for Advanced Education, Victor Valley College District Foundation and regional chambers of commerce.

Since its founding, Comarco Staffing of Victorville has answered employers' needs throughout a decade of record growth. On par with the company's integrity and objective, there is no doubt that Comarco will have continued success as the area's premier personnel service into the next decade and thereafter.

Shear Realty — The Sign of Success

As the project manager for the high desert's Spring Valley Lake planned community, Bob Sher came out from Los Angeles in 1969 with the notion he would stay only until the project's completion. After the success of finalizing a lake, golf course and 4,100 residential lots, Sher seized the opportunity to open his own real estate business.

When Sher staked his first sign in Spring Valley Lake, he was already an experienced real estate professional. His early years in real estate included regional shopping center leasing and site selection, income property sales, and recreational land sales and development. His maternal uncle, Sanford Shear, a longtime Los Angeles real estate broker and developer, became the first broker for Shear Realty. So the story goes concerning the name Bob Sher and Shear Realty.

Bob and Peggy Sher opened their first office in Spring Valley Lake in 1980. Today at the company's Apple Valley headquarters, opened in 1985, Bob serves as founder and president, overseeing all aspects of this thriving real estate operation. Peggy, as treasurer, skillfully handles the firm's financial reins. Shear Realty Vice President Caroll Yule joined the team in 1996 as a partner and vice president in charge of marketing and relocation for the corporation. That same year Leroy and Becky Otwell got their piece of the Shear Realty action. Longtime realtors in the area, the Otwells hung the Shear banner outside their Hesperia office, and as a result are the proud owners and brokers of the company's third location.

Paramount to Shear's philosophy is the practice of linking personal service to the high-end rewards of technical expertise so that technology assists clients' needs in numerous ways. Each of the three offices has a computer center equipped to develop up-to-the-minute market analysis of any property. Additionally, by personal computer anyone can log on to Shear's Web site to research the real estate market in the comfort of their own home. Enhancing this technology is the firm's full complement of 60 professional full-time agents who put a personal touch into each handshake. All of Shear's agents are recruited from the area and are known not only for their accomplishments in real estate but for their knowledge of the community as well.

A strong focus of activities that benefit the community is a point of pride with the firm. Shear actively sponsors such charitable causes as the United Way, The Salvation Army Food Bank, Toys for Tots and High Desert Homeless Services. In addition, of great value to the area is Shear's highly prestigious association with an international relocation company and broker network. With Victor Valley experiencing record growth, Shear works hard to successfully manage employee relocations to and from the region. A Shear relocation specialist aids in the process by preparing a relocation plan customized to the client's individual family or corporate needs.

(Front) Peggy and Bob Sher
(Back, left to right) Becky Otwell, Leroy Otwell and Caroll Yule

It's easy to see how Shear's tradition of pairing industry expertise with personalized consultation has made the Shear Realty sign one of success in Victor Valley and the No.1 company in sales for eight consecutive years since 1992. Furthermore, considering the company's reputation of high integrity it is also easy to believe Bob Sher when he says his company "will remain strongly focused on its vision for growth and exceptional customer service while it leads the way in real estate."

St. Mary Medical Center

Historically, the earliest hospitals limited medical attention to physical ailments. That practice changed dramatically in seventh-century France when St. Landry established the Hotel Dieu Hospital and began addressing the undivided needs of a patient's body, mind and spirit.

Today, at St. Mary Medical Center in Apple Valley, total commitment to every patient's well-being is underscored in all programs and services offered. In harmony with St. Landry's wisdom, and utilizing state-of-the-art technology, St. Mary Medical Center's quality health care defines the spirit of healing exemplary of a modern hospital.

As the Victor Valley's first hospital, St. Mary Medical Center originated in 1954 as the idea of the Desert Valley Hospital Corporation. A groundbreaking ceremony hallmarked the construction period from spring 1955 through October 1956. On November 11, 1956, the hospital's cornerstone was blessed by Bishop Buddy of San Diego and the deed was placed into the welcoming hands of Rev. Mother Regina, Mother General of the Sisters of Immaculate Heart. Under the name of St. Mary Desert Valley Hospital, the 29-bed facility opened its doors on November 19, 1956. Out of the 11 patients received that first day, the very first patient admitted was for maternity services.

Construction of St. Mary Medical Center began in 1955.

In its first year St. Mary employed 51 people, treated 1,130 emergencies, performed 2,772 X-ray exams, performed 640 surgeries and ran 14,031 laboratory tests. By the end of its inaugural year, 1,555 patients had been treated and 361 babies had taken their first breath at St. Mary.

Successful completion of expansion plans in 1958-1959 resulted in the addition of the facility's south wing. This addition of 18 beds increased the hospital's care capacity to 47 beds. In 1959 St. Mary Desert Valley Hospital received the high honor of full accreditation from the Joint Commission on Accreditation for Healthcare Organizations.

Modernization continued through 1968 in order to meet the growing needs of the Victor Valley region. By 1968 an east wing served long-term care patients. The hospital now provided an emergency department, surgery, physical therapy, X-ray and laboratory facilities in addition to a six-bed maternity ward, a six-bed pediatric ward and 55 beds designated for acute medical-surgical patients.

In 1969 hospital sponsorship transferred from the Sisters of Immaculate Heart to the Brothers of St. John of God. Under the guidance of the Brothers of St. John of God, hospital expansion and health care tradition continued hand in hand to answer the needs of the community while ministering to the body, mind and spirit of St. Mary's patients.

The conventions of the Brothers of St. John of God were joined in sponsorship with the Sisters of St. Joseph of Orange in 1992 by way of the prestigious St. Joseph Health System. This transition prompted a name change to St. Mary Regional Medical Center — now known as St. Mary Medical Center.

Progressing from a small facility nearly half a century ago to a comprehensive 186-bed hospital today, St. Mary Medical Center's dedication to serving the public has remained intrinsic to its core value of hospitality expressed through dignity, justice, service and excellence. At the heart of St. Mary's doctrine is its numerous outreach programs. Each year 10 percent of St. Mary's bottom-line revenue is funneled back into community services.

The hospital is shown here in an early photograph.

Leading the list of the medical center's community-based programs is Bright Futures, a 37-foot mobile medical clinic. Bright Futures takes critical health care directly into neighborhoods. A bilingual staff is on hand to answer concerns about health problems, offer guidance concerning doctor referrals and insurance resources, and advise parents about preventative health care, especially immunizations.

Healthy Beginnings and New Avenues are outreach programs providing prenatal care and women's health services through stationary and mobile clinics. Additionally, throughout the year the hospital schedules free screening and low-cost vaccination clinics along with a variety of health education programs. The goal of all of these services is to get quality health care information out to the community in an effort to promote healthier lifestyles.

St. Mary Medical Center is a state-of-the-art health care facility today.

Outpatient care is yet another facet of St. Mary's commitment to providing total health care. Outpatient services include diagnostics tests ranging from computer scans to magnetic resonance imaging that allow doctors to view internally a patient's body without the use of radiation. Therapy programs for physical and occupational rehabilitation along with the service of a speech pathologist are also offered on an outpatient basis, as are some surgical procedures not requiring overnight visitation.

Making so many vital and worthwhile programs and services possible is the supporting mission of the St. Mary Hospital Foundation. The foundation is devoted to providing the financial backbone required to directly pay for remodeling costs, new equipment, construction, in-house services and community programs. In order to accomplish all these objectives, the hospital foundation campaigns arduously through fund-raising activities.

St. Mary Hospital Foundation's ongoing mission includes — at present — the purchase of new ultrasound equipment for the Maternal Child Care Department, a surgical camera for cardiac procedures, cancer detection, imaging equipment and upgrades in the gastrointestinal equipment. Clearly, it is because of the efforts on the part of everyone involved with the St. Mary Hospital Foundation that the financial support for the health care needs of the community today and into the future are realized.

At St. Mary Medical Center, community focus is approached on a person-by-person basis and is everpresent in each aspect of the staff's total-care philosophy. In the spirit of healing, St. Mary staff members provide health care for each patient, addressing and answering patients' needs individually as valued members of the community.

Mohahve Historical Society

Renowned novelist Robert Heinlein once remarked that "A generation which ignores history has no past and no future." Heinlein's observation is an apt subtext that describes the passion and dedication shared by the members of the Mohahve Historical Society (MHS) in their efforts to preserve the past for future generations.

The taproot of the historical society got its start on January 30, 1963, when the Victor Valley College District invited the area's early-day residents to a college-level class about local history. With the sole purpose to compile a history of Victor Valley and the surrounding foothills, a class of 35 students met under the direction of Dr. Lawrence Davenport one week later on February 7th. The following week the class held an old-timers meeting at which long-time residents from Adelanto, Apple Valley, Barstow, Daggett, Helendale, Hesperia, Lucerne Valley, Oro Grande, Phelan, San Bernardino and Victorville showed up with historical photographs and documents in hand. The class went to work sorting the information for the tedious task of recording history. Through personal interviews histories were dictated and recorded. Priceless photos and documents were copied. The hard-earned result of the students' first efforts paid off in June 1963 when *Mohahve I*, a 200-page book, came off the press with 500 copies at $10 each. It sold out immediately. Since the first printing of the Mohahve history series, MHS has produced an additional four books in 1964, 1966, 1984 and 1991.

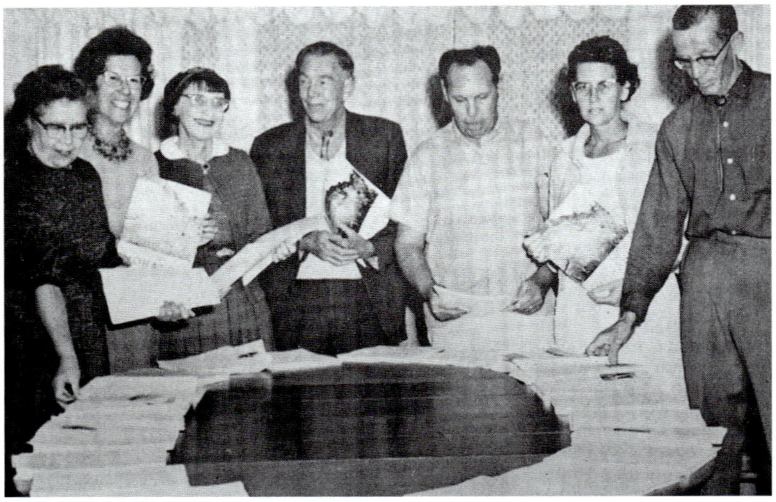

Mohahve Historical Society members of 1964 assemble the second book in the Mohahve series. Left to right are Marjorie Martin, Gladys Steorts, Sylvia Hopping, Paul Hopping, Harold Goldbrandsen Sr., Jean Goldbrandsen and Jack Steorts.

The college didn't offer the class again that year. However, about a dozen students were adamant about carrying on the work. Thus, a local historical society was organized in October 1963 under the title of the Mohahve Association. In 1964 the name was officially changed to the Mohahve Historical Society. Much has been said about the unique spelling of the name Mohahve. The society adopted this form of the name from the diary of John C. Fremont. On his 1844 expedition, Fremont used the spelling of "Mohahve" to identify the native inhabitants and the regional river as well.

In the years following, MHS markedly enhanced the public's knowledge of regional history. Its contributions to preserving history are considerable in nature and scope. MHS was one of the first contributors of cash and artifacts to the Victor Valley Museum. Society members have campaigned via California's Resources Agency to sanction noteworthy points of interest with the placement of historical markers. MHS established a central archival location at the Victor Valley College Library's Local History Collection Center. The society also sponsors numerous publications regarding local history, including its newsletter, *The Mohahve Muse*, and has sponsored a Speakers Bureau for the purpose of sharing history with school and community organizations. Additionally, on its agenda for the future is the creation of a Web page that will make history jump out from the pages of cyber space with the ease of a mouse-click.

Today the Mohahve Historical Society continues to make history a living legacy through an extensive program of collecting and cataloging information, outreach programs involving the recording of oral histories, monthly meetings, field trips and an active membership campaign.

Bibliography

Bean, Lowell J. and Charles R. Smith. *Handbook of the North American Indians* VIII. Smithsonian Institution: Washington D.C., 1978.

Beattie, George William and Helen Pruitt Beattie. *Heritage of the Valley: San Bernardino's First Century.* Biobooks: Oakland, California, 1951.

Bolton, Herbert Eugene, ed. *Font's Complete Diary: A Chronicle of the Founding of San Francisco.* University of California Press: Berkeley, California, 1933.

Brooks, George R., ed. *The Southwest Expedition of Jedediah S. Smith: His Personal Account of the Journey to California, 1826-1827.* University of Nebraska Press: Lincoln, 1977.

Brown, John Jr. and James Boyd, *History of San Bernardino and Riverside County,* 3 vols. Lewis Publishing Co.: Chicago, Illinois, 1922.

Casebier, Dennis G. *Carleton's Pah-Ute Campaign.* Privately printed: Norco, California, 1972.

Dale, Harrison Clifford. *The Ashley-Smith Explorations and the Discovery of a Central Route to the Pacific: 1822-1829.* Arthur H. Clark Company: Glendale, California, 1941.

Desert Evening News, 1851-1900.

Earle, David D. "Serrano Indians." Paper commissioned by and delivered to Victor Valley College lecture series "Exploring the Mojave Desert": September, 1991.

Gillette, J.W. "Some Indian Experiences." *History of Southern California Annual,* 1904.

Hafen, LeRoy R. and Ann W. Hafen. *Journals of the Forty-Niners Salt Lake to Los Angeles.* Arthur H. Clark Company: Glendale, California, 1954.

_______ . *Old Spanish Trail: Santa Fe to Los Angeles.* Arthur H. Clark Company: Glendale, California, 1954.

Jackson, Donald and Mary Lee Spence. *The Expeditions of John Charles Fremont.* University of Illinois Press: Urbana, 1970.

Johnston, Francis J. *The Serrano Indians of Southern California.* Malki Museum Brochure no. 2. Malki Museum Press: Banning, California, 1980.

Los Angeles Star, 1851-1870.

Los Angeles Times, 1894-1930.

Lyman, Edward Leo. "Outmaneuvering the Octopus: Atchison, Topeka and Santa Fe." *California History.* June, 1988.

_______ . "The Arrowhead Trails Highway: California's Predecessor to Interstate 15." *Southern California Historical Quarterly.* Fall, 1999.

Markham, Henry H. Papers. Henry E. Huntington Library and Art Gallery: San Marino, California.

McClure, W.F., J.A. Sourwine, C.E. Tait, *Mojave River Commission Report of the Utilization of Mojave River for Irrigation in Victor Valley, California.* California State Printing Office: Sacramento, 1918.

Mohahve I. Local History Research Project under direction of Lawrence C. Davenport, Victor Valley College, 1963.

Mohahve II-V. Mohahve Historical Society, 1965-1993.

Morgan, Dale L. *Jedediah Smith and the Opening of the West.* University of Nebraska Press: Lincoln, 1953, 1964.

Perris, Frederick T. Letterpress copybooks. Henry E. Huntington Library: San Marino, California.

San Bernardino *Argus,* 1877.

San Bernardino *Courier,* 1886-1893.

San Bernardino *Daily Times-Index,* 1875-1898.

San Bernardino *Guardian,* 1867-1874.

San Bernardino *Sun,* 1895-1940.

San Bernardino Valley *Index,* 1881.

Strong, William Duncan. *Aboriginal Society in Southern California.* Reprint of 1929 University of California publication. Malki Museum Press: Banning and Riverside, California, 1987.

Thompson, David G. *The Mojave Desert Region, California: A Geographic, Geologic and Hydrologic Reconnaissance.* United States Government Printing Office: Washington D.C., 1929.

Thompson, Richard D. and Katherine Thompson. *Pioneer of the Mojave: The Life and Times of Aaron G. Lane.* Privately printed: Victorville, California, 1995.

Thompson, Richard D. ed., "Silas C. Cox: Daniel Boone of the West, Life History, Second Version." *San Bernardino County Museum Quarterly,* Fall, 1974.

Transcript of oral interviews conducted with Victor Valley residents by Rev. Paul Smith, Leo Lyman and Victor Valley College students, Fran Elgin and other members of the Mohahve Historical Society. Victor Valley College Library Local History Collection.

Victor Valley *News Herald,* 1913-1945.

Victorville *Daily Press,* 1935-1990.

Vredenburgh, Larry H., Gary L. Shumway and Russell D. Hartill, *Desert Fever: An Overview of Mining in the California Desert.* Living West Press: Conoga Park, California, 1981.

Walker, Clifford J. *Back Door to California: The Story of the Mojave River Trail.* Mojave River Valley Museum Association: Barstow, California, 1986.

Index

Partners Index

Santa Fe